Project evaluation

ENGINEERING MANAGEMENT

Series editor   S. H. Wearne, BSc(Eng), PhD, FICE, Consultant, Director of Institution courses and in-company training

Editorial panel   D. E. Neale, CEng, FICE; D. P. Maguire, BSc, CEng, FICE; D. J. Ricketts, BSc, CEng, MICE; J. V. Tagg, CEng, FICE; G. D. Cottam, BSc(Eng), CEng, FICE; J. C. Bircumshaw, BSc, CEng, MICE

Other titles in the series
Civil engineering insurance and bonding, P. Madge
Marketing of engineering services, J. B. H. Scanlon
Civil engineering contracts, S. H. Wearne
Managing people, A. S. Martin and F. Grover (Eds)
Management of design offices, P. A. Rutter and A. S. Martin (Eds)
Control of engineering projects, S. H. Wearne (Ed)
Construction planning, R. H. Neale and D. E. Neale
Financial control, N. M. L. Barnes (Ed)
Principles of engineering organization, S. H. Wearne

ENGINEERING MANAGEMENT

Project evaluation

Edited by
R. K. Corrie, BA, BAI, MICE, CEng, FBIM
W. S. Atkins Project Management

Thomas Telford Ltd, London

Published by Thomas Telford Ltd, Thomas Telford House,
1 Heron Quay, London E14 9XF

First published 1991

British Library Cataloguing in Publication Data
Project evaluation
  1. Engineering. Projects. Management
  I. Corrie, R. K.   II. Series
  620.0068

ISBN 0 7277 1384 1

Printed and bound in Great Britain by
Mackays of Chatham PLC, Chatham, Kent

Foreword

This book is aimed primarily at mid-career engineers. The objective is to provide a background to the important non-technical strategic, organisational and other issues, essential to project initiation and success, in which they will increasingly find themselves involved. For accountants and others who become involved in projects, it provides an insight into the project development process.

In addition to the process of project appraisal and feasibility study normally carried out as a prerequisite to project initiation, the evaluation of project performance during implementation is included. All stages of project evaluation from conception to commissioning are covered — however, the aim is not to provide a text book on how to manage and execute a project, but rather to set out a summary of activities, procedures and controls which a reviewer would expect to find in place at each stage of the development of a well-run project. Potential problem areas are highlighted and key performance elements listed.

For those who wish to examine specific topics more closely, a list of suggested further reading is included.

Acknowledgements

The author is indebted to all of his colleagues at W S Atkins who contributed ideas, text and comment towards the production of this book. In particular he would like to thank Neil Tolan for his work in completing the first draft, Michael Burke for rewriting and rationalising the final text and Bob Thomas for his enthusiastic support and help throughout.

Contents

1 Introduction

1.1 Subject and structure

This book is concerned with the evaluation of a project, and the factors that affect its outcome at each stage in its life cycle. It covers both project feasibility appraisal and the subsequent review of the whole or part of a project to check that the plans and performance are capable of achieving the objectives. Such reviews should be a regular feature in the monitoring of major or lengthy projects.

The term 'project' could mean almost any set of planned actions — here, we concentrate on capital investment projects. Typically, these result in the creation of new industrial facilities, modifications of existing ones, works of building construction, or civil engineering works for transport and infrastructure. A wide variety of situations in terms of size, complexity and technical requirements may be involved — as we also have to take into account such other variable factors as location and the aims and organisation of the promoting party, it is clear that each project constitutes a 'one-off' task, with its own peculiarities. Nevertheless, general procedures relating to the methods of evaluation can be applied to most projects.

The conduct of project evaluation and review entails partly the use of precise techniques and partly skill, which can only be learnt by practice. In this book the approaches to project evaluation and their implementation are discussed, in the belief that this will prove more helpful than attempts at prescriptions or ready-made solutions.

As for presentation, there are some common factors despite the disarray created by the variety of project situations. For example, although the paths of development differ in detail from project to project, the overall pattern is the same in most cases; a sequence of phases is followed, from planning through design, procurement and construction to commissioning, as shown in Fig. 1.1.

1

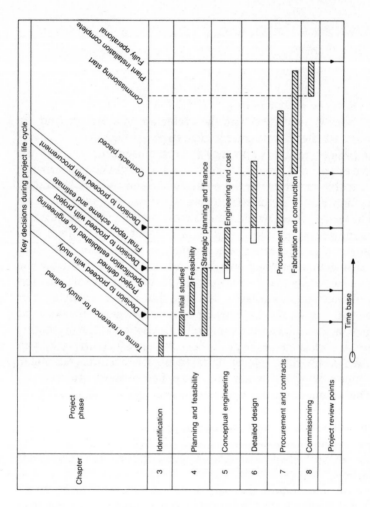

Fig. 1.1 Typical stages of a project

Although the phases are sometimes overlapped or merged, this sequence represents a common structure which has been used in arranging the main chapters. Chapter 2 indicates the participants in a project; each of the chapters from 3 to 8 deals with one of the six project phases, from identification through to commissioning. Formal project reviews are discussed in chapter 9.

Types of project evaluation

Three types of evaluation are identified, namely:

- planning and feasibility studies
- in-project evaluation during implementation
- project performance reviews.

The planning and feasibility phase is usually the first complete evaluation of a project. The aim is to consider and compare the possible courses of action, and to select that which best meets the stated objectives. The result should be a well-defined project proposal, with a broad plan for its implementation. The plan should prove the project's financial and technical viability, outline the facilites to be constructed and installed, and establish the cost and time required to complete the project.

Some engineers and managers consider a project to start only when a basic objective and scope of work have been defined, i.e. when the feasibility stage is finished and an instruction has been given to proceed with the design; some would place the start point even later. In this book the project is considered to exist at a much earlier stage, for two reasons. First, the feasibility studies are highly significant in terms of evaluation, although they take place before the design proper commences. Second, the causes of project failures occurring during implementation or after completion can often be traced back to deficiencies in the planning stages. Thus, the process of evaluation involved in the project identification and feasibility study phases is described in some detail in chapters 3 and 4.

In-project evaluation during implementation

In-project evaluation is one of the tasks of project management during each phase and when approaching points of decision, approval or change. The purpose is to ascertain whether or not the project is deviating from its chosen course and time schedule, and if so, for what reason; sometimes while the project is on course

3

changing circumstances require some adjustment to be considered. In either case the aim is to initiate any necessary corrective action. As part of this evaluation, the project manager must be able to review a set of project data and extract the salient facts. Sometimes presented data may be of doubtful validity — the project manager must test such information and learn how to recognise potential problems and their causes.

In-project evaluation during the design and implementation phases is dealt with in chapters 5–8. Because of the nature of the work, the treatment in these chapters differs from that of the previous phases. Each chapter describes briefly the activities of project development normally carried out in the particular phase; then, at appropriate points, that phase is examined from the point of view of a person outside the project making a review of performance with a specific check list. This also gives insights into the sort of questions the project manager should be asking in his own evaluation process. At the end of each chapter is a short list of review topics for the phase, which experience shows should be considered by a reviewer. These lists are not intended to be exhaustive.

Project performance reviews

These are formal reviews conducted for a specific reason. They are frequently executed by specialists not directly engaged in the projects. Project performance reviews may be requested or initiated by the Client, by some external interested party such as a funding agency, or by the project manager. The purpose is to make a 'stand-off' evaluation of all aspects of a project which may affect its outcome, and to recommend how any deficiencies in the plans or performance can be rectified.

Such reviews would be expected to take place during later phases of problem projects — however, most problems have their origin in the early stages of project development, and maximum benefits can be obtained from reviews carried out in the setting-up phases. Project performance reviews form the subject of chapter 9.

1.2 General comments

Discussion of evaluation in this book centres on large or complex projects, as these are usually subject to a wide range of internal and external influences. Internal factors include the way a project

4

is organised and the criteria for judging the achievement of objectives. The latter are, or can be, reduced to a combination of time, cost and quality targets. External influences can be numerous, including in the feasibility phase for example land use, planning, environmental, social impact, infrastructural, political and public interest assessments, as well as technical aspects. Smaller projects are frequently subject to the same influences.

In practice, the effects of external factors are more evident now than in the past, especially the higher level of attention now accorded to environmental protection and social impact. Indeed, smaller projects can easily run into difficulties because they are perceived by those responsible as being relatively simple and compactly organised, without too many participants — 'everyone knows what they are doing'. Alas, history shows that this is not always the case, so the principles and general rules of project evaluation should be applied to small projects as well as large ones.

In considering the approaches to project evaluation, we must remember that every project is dynamic and continually changing as the development proceeds. Project Management is often said to be the management of change, as the purpose of a project is to plan and implement change of one sort or another. In another sense, however, 'the management of change' should be applied to the work in the project itself — as its character changes from one phase of development to the next, the need to change the organisation of the work to suit each phase must be recognised and anticipated. Project evaluation and review, therefore, should always be forward-looking.

2 Participants in a project

2.1 Introduction

A project is influenced by the participating parties and their interrelationship. These can represent many interests and requirements, all of which must be satisfied to a greater or lesser extent. While project evaluation should deal with facts and figures, the people involved can also influence the result, particularly where matters of opinion or value judgements arise.

Participants in a project can be classified as follows:

- 'directly involved' participants include all those who are employed full-time or part-time in the project organisation, with responsibility for planning and implementation
- 'indirectly involved' participants are usually part of the Client organisation but not directly involved in the project from day to day; for example, operations and maintenance departments as users, commercial management and corporate planners
- 'external' participants are those who have a real or perceived interest in the project, for example from a financial or environmental impact point of view.

Figure 2.1 shows relationships between direct, indirect and external parties, and the interests and extended lines of communication that may result from their involvement. This chapter provides some pointers to possible characteristics and motivations of the various parties, to help in understanding their likely roles.

2.2 Direct participants
The Client

For the purposes of this book, the Client is the body responsible for making decisions on the development of the project. In a variety

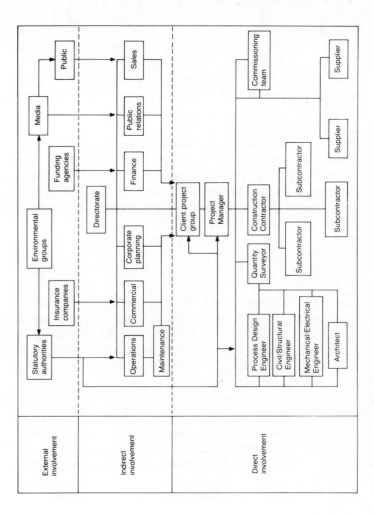

Fig. 2.1. Participants in a project

of contexts there may also be funding agencies, promoter, developer, sponsor and user, each of which may exercise, in whole or in part, the functions of initiating, financing and supporting the project. For simplicity, we will use the single term 'the Client' to encompass all these parties, while bearing in mind their interrelationships.

The Client may be an individual, such as a promoter, who will reserve to himself the making of all important decisions; or it may be an organisation acting through nominated representatives. The Client organisation comprises several functions through which its work is executed, and these are found in some form in the public sector and in commerical companies. Fig. 2.1 shows a possible organisation for a commercial company as an example for discussion. Here, the project group is a section or department whose job it is to deal with the project or projects — it has an executive role and reports to the Directorate of the company. This group is the only direct participant in the Client's office; its leader is responsible for implementing the Directors' policy. People performing other functions, such as operations and commercial personnel, are indirect participants, as they have only an advisory role to the project and are sources of information, as shown in section 2.3.

Figure 2.1 may appear strange because it is a distortion of the company structure, with the project placed at the centre. In reality, the project team would be only a single function among others of equal or greater importance in the company as a whole. The function labelled 'operations', for example, would be a central feature exercised by an executive department in line mangement. Others, such as corporate planning or public relations, would be placed much as shown here.

Not all companies have a project department, and many other types of organisation are encountered. Suffice it to say, for the present, that the type and structure of the Client company can influence the conduct of the early or planning phases, and must be understood. This will predetermine or at least influence the following questions.

- How is the project organised?
- Who will be the participants?
- What will be their responsibilities?

8

- What are the criteria for feasibility?
- What will be the priorities for re-evaluation or redirection (if necessary during implementation)?

In practice, the Client in each situation will have its own particular characteristics and influence; it is not helpful to catergorise them too firmly or to attach too many labels. However, using some labels, such as the Client's role as an *operator*, does help our understanding:

- primary operator — this term is used to convey the direct linkage of the project to the Client's fundamental reason for existence — a new manufacturing plant or product line, for example
- secondary operator — in this case the Client will operate the facilities when they are completed, but they will be incidental to his main production activity — a new corporate headquarters for an industrial organisation, for example.
- non-operator — a Client who does not intend to use the end result of the project himself, such as a property developer who is having a building constructed for lease or sale.

A primary operator will typically have a far greater technical input into the project than a secondary operator, and will be likely to define his requirements in some detail and to perform more studies and evaluations utilising in-house resources. Furthermore, a primary operator with a continuing capital investment programme will have a clearer understanding of project development than one with no such experience. In contrast, a non-operator such as a property developer may not have technical expertise in-house but will exercise close control in financial matters.

Other relevant factors that may influence the Client's approach can be represented by some examples. Government bodies are subject to different constraints from most commercial organisations because of public accountability and bureaucracy; prolonged decision-making procedures can result. Commercial companies, on the other hand, are more likely to expedite their decisions, particularly where time is of the essence in achieving the project objectives.

However, in some larger organisations there may be structural constraints which cause the responsibility for decision-making to be diffused. In a recent situation, the in-house project manager of a large industrial company was provided with a project advisory group drawn from 'indirect participants', including representatives of production, estimating, cost control and engineering functions. Such groups can be exceedingly useful in communications, in keeping interested departments in touch with progress, and in enabling the user and operational departments to become familiar with the project. In this case, however, the major project was being controlled as an item of the Client's normal operations and cost control arrangements. Consequently, the advisers were also acting as controllers, using their own departmental procedures. Because these were inappropriate for a construction project, frustration and delays resulted. In short, the Client's organisation and approach are ineluctable facts whose impact should never be ignored.

The project manager

The term 'project manager' has become overworked — each participating party may have one or several persons so titled, who may only be responsible for certain elements. In this book the term is used to signify that person who has overall or principal responsibility for the management of the project as a whole. The project manager plans the work, monitors and directs the participants, and seeks to ensure that the project is completed on schedule, within budget and to the required quality.

In practice, the project manager may be a member of the Client's staff and may be in an executive position in the organisation, as in Fig. 2.1. Alternatively, he or she may be a separate appointee with no direct responsibility for design or construction, as shown in Fig. 2.2, being rather in an overseeing and liaison role. Such a concept, common in some industrial sectors, is beneficial where there are a large number of participating companies and complex interfaces. This type of project manager is usually an individual or organisation having a predominantly technical background, with experience in multidisciplinary projects. But whatever the type of appointment, the project manager's position and authority should meet the above definition; if not, the position will be ineffective.

Historically, many large projects have been run without appointment of a project manager, either because the Client retained this control or because it was delegated to 'the Engineer' or 'the Architect' engaged for the design. The terms of the standard professional Agreements included both the design and some

10

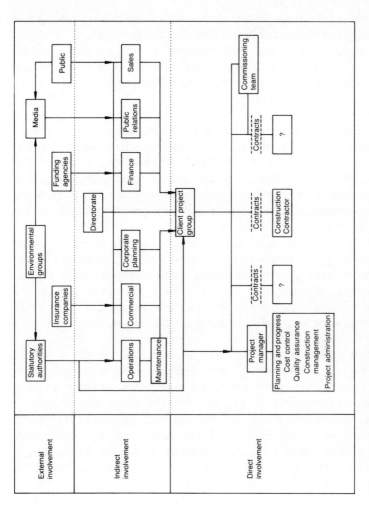

Fig. 2.2. Participants in a project (alternative)

supervisory functions in respect of the construction contracts. This pattern is changing as a result of increased use of fee competition. At the same time, project management has been recognised as a necessary function.

Most people are aware of the role of the project manager as distinct, for example, from that of a design leader. The project manager's role should also be distinguished from that of the Client (who is initiator and paymaster), even in cases where project management is a part-time in-house function.

The designers

One or more organisations may be responsible for the design. These are usually grouped by technical specialisation rather than by area or phase of a project. The design work may be undertaken by the Client, consulting engineers, architectural practices, engineering contractors or construction contractors' technical departments. The design team may be supported by independent or in-house quantity surveyors.

The designers may become involved at the feasibility stage; sometimes they may even initiate the project and then seek a Client. Various arrangements commonly used for design work are discussed in later chapters. The design leader is the principal technical participant, and should be carefully selected for technical competence and ability to mangage the design team.

The Contractor

The Contractor (or Contractors) is, perhaps rather loosely, defined as the organisation which undertakes the construction at site. Engineers will be familiar with the wide range of types of contract. At one extreme, a Turnkey Contractor may be responsible for planning and design as well as procurement and construction, particularly if he is a joint sponsor or initiator of the project, as for the Channel Tunnel. At the other extreme, he may simply be employed by the Client to provide labour to erect or install the Client's own equipment: in between lies a wide range of management contracts with or without subsupplier and subcontract arrangements.

Types of contract and their implications are discussed in chapter 5.

Vendor or supplier

A vendor or supplier is one who supplies materials or equipment manufactured away from the project work site. He may also install and commission them at the site. Materials and equipment, their sources and available options for supply, may be important factors in evaluation. The logistics of the project are greatly influenced by suppliers; the planning, inspection and direction of supplies and suppliers are fundamental tasks for the project management team.

2.3 Indirect participants

Most of this group (see Fig. 2.1) form part of the Client's organisation but are not concerned with the project from day to day and are not directly responsible for it. They provide input at all stages and may monitor its progress. These participants are listed below, with an indication of their potential influence. For present purposes they are identified as found in a large commercial company.

Directorate

As the Directors are responsible for overall policy and direction of the Client's business, they will:

- make the decision to proceed with the project at each stage
- approve major changes, particularly those involving increased funding.

Operations

- May identify the need for a project, particularly in relation to improving the efficiency of the production process
- has major input into planning and layout of design
- must maintain close liaison at all stages of the project
- is the 'customer' for the project, but not for the service or product derived therefrom.

Finance

- Establishes that funds are available for the project from internal or external resources
- monitors cash flow
- audits overall project costs on a regular basis.

Corporate planning
- Evaluates the project in terms of its overall compatability with the aims of the Directorate
- has a significant input into the initial stages up to the decision to proceed, but thereafter has limited involvement in the implementation phases.

Sales (marketing)
- May provide impetus for the project by identifying the need for the product or facility
- provides data defining customer requirements
- advises as to when the product or facility should be available.

Public relations
- May advise at the concept and feasibility stages
- provides liaison and dissemination of information during implementation
- has a significant role for projects with high profile and/or major environmental implications.

Personnel department and trade unions
Provide consultation and advice on the availability of the workforce with the right skills and on provision for training; project feasibility and economic viability may depend upon attitudes and acceptance of working practices and associated issues.

2.4 External participants
The set of external participants, who are not involved in project implementation but have a real or perceived interest in it, comprises statutory authorities, funding agencies and unofficial groups.

Statutory authorities
These are parties from whom the Client (or sometimes the Contractors) must seek various consents and approvals, especially in the planning stages. A Government Department or other authority may be the Client, as mentioned above, but it is its statutory or regulating role that is dealt with here.

The situation varies from country to country. For an overseas project, the laws and procedures of the country concerned must be observed, with the added complexities of international trading.

It is commonly the case that the overseas Client will offload all responsibility for meeting legal, fiscal and other statutory requirements by making it a contractual obligation on the Consultant or Contractor to observe all laws and regulations and obtain all necessary statutory approvals for the project. The following paragraphs provide an outline of the UK situation, as being of interest to many engineers.

Planning applications and consent in the UK are primarily administered by the local authority in whose area the site of the project lies. In general, the authority is the District Council, which is responsible for detailed local planning, while the County Council is responsible for broad strategic planning.

The powers of the councils are derived from legislation such as the 1971 Town and Country Planning Act and the several more recent Local Government Acts. However, the relationships between local and central government are complex. The Government can, through legislation, increase or decrease the level of local control, and can also interfere with planning matters. It can act as the higher appeal authority in the case of objections, or influence local levels of resources, and thus withold or grant planning approvals.

In the event of a public inquiry, an Inspector is usually appointed by the Department of the Environment to conduct the proceedings and to produce the report which will decide the issue. Depending on the nature and aims of the project, other Ministries may also be concerned — the Department of Energy and the Department of Trade, for example.

While the delicate balance between central and local authority can change according to the national policy of the Government of the day, the means of operation of both are affected increasingly by European Community (EC) standards and legislation, which already have a bearing on land use, environmental protection and standards, technical specifications, safety and working conditions.

There are also the numerous public sector agencies responsible for providing public facilities and service. Some of these, although in public (State) ownership at present, are subject to changes of status and organisation. These agencies naturally initiate and conduct their own projects, undertake developments jointly with commercial organisations in some cases, and influence the planning scene in many ways. Apart from Government Departments, the main group is the Statutory Undertakings. These include the

15

agencies responsible for electricity, gas and water supply and distribution, drainage and sewerage, communications and transport (e.g. British Rail, the Civil Aviation Authority and the Post Office), which provide essential services to projects and may also be responsible for indirect planning constraints arising from their own plans of development.

An important statutory body is the Health and Safety Executive, which, with its staff of inspectors, has wide powers over the whole field of health and safety at work, both in factories and on construction sites. Numerous other agencies, such as those concerned with heritage and environment matters, may influence projects. These are not necessarily statutory bodies. It is necessary to understand the powers and procedures of any authorities and agencies that may be involved, and to consult them at the right time and in the right way.

Funding agencies

Commercial banks, insurance companies, the World Bank, the Asian Development Bank etc. act as sources of loan capital. Grants may also be made available in various ways from government, the EC, the Export Credits Guarantee Department (for exports) and local authorities. Any of these can impose conditions that affect project feasibility and implementation; they may also insist on the adoption of particular contract strategies.

Unofficial groups

These external participants are a source of increasing influence, whose role can sometimes impinge on a project in surprising ways. In most cases their interest can be expressed in the planning phases, largely in terms of environmental and social impact (to be discussed in chapter 4). This in turn may affect project costs by way of environmental treatment, compensation, or otherwise. Naturally, these groups have needs to be considered, but in many instances their intervention has made a positive contribution to the project. They comprise:

- people directly affected — local residents, landowners and land users including farmers
- trade associations

- pressure groups — not personally affected but having an interest, often concerned with environmental impact.

Where objections to a project are publicly voiced, the resolution of the issues often rests with the planning authority, which must determine the balance between disadvantages, such as environmental damage, and the benefits associated with the proposals. However, the need for adequate consultation is self-evident nowadays, as a result of the transformation which has taken place in attitude of both the Government and the public.

2.5 Review topics
A review, at any stage, should consider such questions as the following.

- Have all participants and parties who may have an interest in the project been identified?
- Have their roles and their involvement been defined?
- Has each party been adequately briefed on the project (including the involvement of others)?
- Are methods of communication adequate (including procedures for exchange of information)?
- What risks to the project arise from the involvement of the various parties? Have the risks been considered in terms of time and cost? (For example the possible delay and cost associated with archaeological or environmental investigations.)

3 Project identification phase

3.1 Introduction

The project identification phase comprises the preliminary appraisal of a potential project. The aim is to decide whether a feasibility study should be undertaken and, if so, to define the project objectives and the ground rules for the study. In this chapter the preliminary appraisal process, which should be regarded as an evaluation even though it is preproject, is described. The appraisal is the first, formative, stage leading to the implementation of the project, and usually conditions the end result. As mentioned in chapter 1, it is important to establish correctly the aims of the potential project and the criteria to be used to judge solutions.

The preliminary appraisal should follow the lines of Fig. 3.1. The elements to be examined are in general the same as those which would be considered in the subsequent feasibility study (chapter 4); i.e. market demand, technical, economic, environmental and financial factors, etc. In this preliminary phase, however, the studies should be in outline only. All the steps in Fig. 3.1 are covered in the following sections, although for convenience of description the headings are slightly different.

The descriptions in this chapter are brief, as the topics are covered in more detail in the feasibility study. In particular, certain definitions and the details of methods of evaluation are held over to chapter 4. However, section 3.8 deals generally with risk analysis and includes a review of the techniques available and their applicability at various stages.

The origins of projects are either related to a recognised set of problems or derived from opportunity. In the first group are public sector projects such as the second Severn Crossing, which emerge as a result of immediate or predicted needs. In fact the needs may be of long standing, as priorities and hence the timing of public sector projects result from continual juggling with the funds available. These are never sufficient to meet all needs and are affected by the political climate and will. In the private sector also many projects arise from a perceived need, for the expansion or modernisation of plant capacity, for example.

Projects derived from business opportunities require a different approach. Making the most of opportunities is the role of the

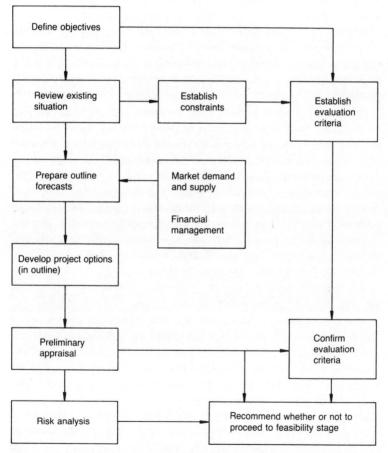

Fig. 3.1. Steps in project identification

entrepreneur, and demands insights which cannot be obtained simply by analytical study of problems and the existing situation. Such insight can lead to successful exploitation of an opportunity simply by good timing and intelligent deployment of 'the three Ms' — men, money and management. On the other hand, to convert ideas into profitable business, a project with different characteristics from those of a standard problem solving scheme may be required — an innovative approach can call for existing forms of development in a new location or in a novel association, or can arise from applying new technology.

As far as new technology is concerned, governments have a long history of involvement in projects that explore technological frontiers, mostly in defence or in the public utility industries. These projects are usually one-off, do not develop through the normal sequence of stages, and are subject to numerous iterations and loops, particularly during their (usually prolonged) design process.

Research-led projects can hardly be subjected to estimating and cost control in the conventional sense, as neither the end results nor the time required to produce them can be predicted. Projects that involve substantial technical development show some of the same characteristics, although the design goal may be more specific. Control is usually exercised on a time and resources basis. In such design/development contracts, for the Government for example, both parties try to contain risk by building deliverables into the contract such that intermediate products are identified at each step, tied to agreed time and cost limits. These specialised means of control and evaluation are outside the scope of this book.

The effects of rapid technological change, however, cannot be ignored. The design of products, equipment and services that are 'current' at the start of project design may be outdated by the time the project is commissioned. Computers provide one example — projects which are heavily dependent on computerised systems for their operation, such as a national library, are vulnerable to changes in physical planning, staffing and other factors, occasioned by the rapid development of systems design. In the field of health care, the pace of development of medical equipment and procedures has similar effects on hospital projects. The impact on physical planning, cost and time must be provided for, particularly in projects having a long gestation period.

20

A project exists not just from the time that design is started, but from the much earlier point at which someone says: 'We should have a look at putting a new facility in at X'. The first step is to define the objectives.

3.2 Project objectives
Definition

The project objectives are conditioned by the Client's strategic aims. Even when these appear to be obvious — for example the profits and long term health of a company, or implementation of Government policy — they should be reviewed to ensure that the project objectives are consistent with them.

The project objectives should be written down concisely and stated unequivocally. There may be one or two principal objectives and a number of subsidiary aims. Effort at the beginning to clarify these will pay dividends later. The objectives do not necessarily have to remain fixed for all time — they can be adjusted in the light of subsequent developments and information — but confusion over them is likely to render decision-making on investment particularly difficult.

Experience of project evaluation and review has shown how often these issues are clouded and left unclarified, with near-fatal results later. Sometimes the basic objectives are laid down too tightly and inflexibly, remaining unchangeable despite changing conditions and new information later in the development. In cases where the Client is a corporation, even one experienced in development, it may be difficult to establish the exact source of authority to make decisions. Sometimes, because of conflict between departments, the objectives and terms of reference handed to external organisations for preparation of a feasibility stage are incomplete, resulting in delays and abortive work.

Defining 'the real Client' is not always easy. For example, on a technically straightforward factory project or a town-centre development, the Client may be some form of *ad hoc* partnership of the statutory authority, one or more funding agencies, and a developer.

The solution lies in understanding the Client organisation and the relationships between the participants and their functions. The preliminary appraisal should address such questions as the following.

21

- In what form can the objectives (which will frame the project) be expressed concisely and unequivocally?
- Which parts of the aims are reserved for later definition?
- How do the various participants relate, and what are their functions?
- How can the work of the feasibility stage help to resolve conflicting aims?

Occasions arise, particularly in the public sector, where a number of objectives are in conflict. As a simple example — a proposed power station may be built, but only at the expense of environmental damage. The project has to be developed with all the objectives in mind. In order that the appraisal process may reflect the priorities attached to the different aims, these should always be discussed with the Client and confirmed.

Conditions and constraints

It is very rare for a project not to be constrained in some way. A constraint is an upper limit to the availability of some necessary resource, such as:

- capital investment
- level of annual operating expenditure
- personnel requirements (trained staff can be scarce)
- supplies, e.g. building materials, power, water.

These conditions, however, are not the only ones. A project must be viewed in relation to its surroundings, and particularly the external influences which may be present, as shown in the example given in Fig. 3.2. Some of these may be difficult to quantify at this stage, but the earlier they are identified and their effects described the less likely they are to cause unpleasant surprises later.

Criteria

The criteria to be used in the subsequent preliminary appraisal should also be settled beforehand. These are of two kinds — the project objectives and the measures or units of comparison.

The main project objectives are obviously necessary conditions which any development plan must fulfil. Normally, several such plans would be considered (these will be termed 'options' — see section 3.5). Each of the plans may fulfil the objectives to a different

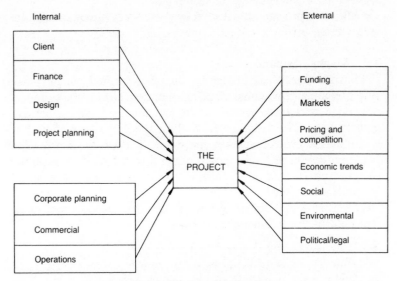

Fig. 3.2. The project and its surroundings

extent and in a different way. For a manufacturing project, for example, the options may not produce the same ranges or volumes of products; this should be taken into account in the appraisal. Other criteria that are frequently relevant are of the following types.

● Economic	Net present value (NPV)
	Internal rate of return (IRR)
● Financial	Return
	Capital cost
	Recurrent cost
● Environmental	Impact assessment
	(air, noise, visual, landscape and
	chemical pollution)
● Social	Impact assessment
● Political	

The criteria are influenced by the legal framework, for example the EC legislation on the environmental acceptability of some classes of industrial development, which requires that impact statements be prepared to a specified standard.

Social impact is increasingly recognised as a factor to be weighed in decisions, particularly for projects in developing countries. In

23

the UK most projects are affected by statutory planning procedures (see section 3.6).

3.3 Market demand

The objectives of the project having been clarified, the next task is to prepare a provisional assessment of demand for the products or services which the project would provide, and the competitive environment. The details of the analysis should be quantified. For an industrial project, market analysis will reveal the scope for a new production unit or a new product line, whereas for a public sector infrastructure project an analysis of need is usually required in the first instance.

The first step should be to study the existing situation, particularly the following questions.

- How is existing demand being met?
- How are existing facilities performing?
- What is the condition of existing facilities?
- What are the likely levels of future demand?

Forecasts of future demand are usually projections based on an analysis of present demand for certain products or of unfulfilled needs; the forecasts should cover the proposed 'project life' whether it be 10, 20 or 30 years. For small scale private sector projects of relatively short life, or major infrastructure projects with up to 30 years of life, the broad future level of demand is essential background to option formulation.

3.4 Financial management

The Client must formulate his thoughts on project financing, as the financial conditions will affect the possible options from the beginning. Questions which should be answered include the following.

- What are the sources of funding?
- What criteria or rules apply?
- How could the project best respond to those rules?

Typically, UK Government projects draw their funds from the Treasury, although in recent years there has been a trend to mixed financing. In funding private sector developments there are grants and fiscal benefits to be considered. In developing countries the multilateral lending agencies may be involved; if so, their requirements must be taken into account and discussions opened.

The financial performance of existing facilities associated with the project should be examined, and the present problems analysed. Projects can be designed to exploit opportunities or to correct and overcome deficiencies; preventing further losses can be as important a financial contribution as generating new profits. In short, the financial context should be examined and its effects understood. In addition to project financing, the control of project costs should be considered (see section 3.6).

3.5 Options

The next step is to define the project itself on the basis of the work described above. A convenient way to proceed is to devise various project options (in concept), each meeting the objectives, and then compare them. An 'option' for present purposes is a written statement defining a development by capital investment to meet the need or exploit the perceived opportunity.

For projects in the public eye, the production of several possible solutions is essential to cover the ground and anticipate possible objections. On the other hand, if the objective is to exploit an opportunity, and the Client feels that he knows the answer already, he may also feel that too much time spent in analytical study may result in the opportunity slipping away from him. In such a case he may state his objectives in terms of one option only.

So why use options and comparisons at all? One reason is to make sure that no attractive scheme goes unrecognised — a wise precaution to take at this stage, when it costs very little to think about it. A second reason is that using an orderly and organised method of evaluation, taking all factors into account, is much more likely to result in success because it will reveal the relative strengths, weaknesses and potential problems of various solutions. It is not suggested that time should be wasted searching blind alleys, but rather that the main possibilities should be considered. A reminder is apposite that even during a short design and construction schedule of 1–2 years, the surroundings (Fig. 3.2) may change surprisingly quickly, as do people's attitudes — what seems attractive today may be less so in the changed conditions of a year from now.

The options or schemes can be devised as follows.

25

- Consider the factors which may affect the options, such as:
  - site location
  - site or plant internal layout
  - human resources
  - materials, energy and other physical resources
  - possible levels of investment
  - likely types and scale of process
  - capital and operating costs
  - phasing of investment.

- Select a limited number of options, differing genuinely in terms of the most important factors.
- Provide information for preliminary appraisal of the options.

Each option should be identified by a description, usually in the following terms:

- the location, with an outline physical plan of facilities
- the type, range and volume of products to be made or services to be provided by the new facilities
- technical features, and the process design to be employed
- order of capital cost
- a statement of the economic benefits that are likely to be created
- the environmental treatment likely to be required
- the planning status of the proposed development.

The description is simply a method of clarifying what each option comprises, so that it can be appraised as precisely as possible.

Finally, the question 'What if we carry on as we are?' should always be considered. It is often helpful to evaluate this course and its consequences, termed the 'do-nothing option', in parallel with the development options.

3.6 Preliminary appraisal
Purpose

The purpose of this appraisal of the options should be to review their characteristics and the extent to which they can fulfil the objectives, as a basis for deciding which schemes should be further examined in the next phase. There are seven main topics to be covered, as described below.

Technical assessment

Each option should be examined to determine whether or not it will work technically. For a manufacturing project, questions are asked such as whether or not the technology is completely established, what size/capacity units are involved, and whether or not material and process flow can be sketched out. Whether an option involves novel techniques or state-of-the-art methods, the probability of their success or failure should be assessed.

The financial risk inherent in an option involving novel techniques should be covered by including a risk provision; an option using only proven technology will be more predictable. This is an example of the way that various criteria and influences interact — in this case technical data, cost and time. It is a matter of judgement whether or not each option is an effective technical solution worthy of inclusion in the next phase.

Financial assessment

Outline costs for each option should always be produced, taking into account the whole development period up to and including commissioning. These costs are usually based on historical data for similar projects, with suitable factors applied, and are only 'order of magnitude' — indeed, they should be in the form of a range of estimates rather than a single figure. Their accuracy is usually inadequate for production of reliable discounted cash flows and financial analyses, but they should be used for calculating preliminary cash flows, perhaps in conjunction with historical cash flow profiles for similar situations.

The income generated by each project option is assessed and the financial position estimated. Both revenues and costs are assembled based on values at a common base date; prices and the value of money are kept constant.

Options which cannot produce sufficient income to cover their costs are likely to be dropped at this point, unless political factors override such considerations. For many public sector projects it is not possible to develop an income forecast, and decisions are made on economic rather than financial criteria.

Economic benefits

The economic assessment is concerned with the worth of each option to the community at large, not just with financial income or cost to the developer or user. Financial and economic evaluation is discussed in more depth in chapter 4 and in appendix A. For the time being, note that in this preliminary assessment the economic benefits and associated costs should be calculated year by year, so that the difference between them can be established. As with financial calculation, the assessment should be used in comparing options, but is not normally sufficiently accurate to be used for absolute values.

Project planning assessment

Project planning in this context means scheduling of time and resources. At this stage, project planning is used as a decision support tool rather than one of project control, and therefore an outline form is adequate, appropriate to the limitations of the available information.

An outline plan should be prepared for each option, taking into account such fundamental points as the following.

- Is there sufficient definition of the project scope to estimate time on a factored basis from experience on other similar projects?
- What factors (funding, technical development, materials or labour supply, etc.) dictate the pace of the project, and are they manageable?
- What major risks are inherent in the project concept, and have they been taken into account in the planning stage?

Risk analysis techniques are commonly used to assist in establishing the degree of uncertainty that the funding agency or client is prepared to accept in the estimates of time and cost. The old method of 'adding a bit here and there just in case' is not sufficient for the project environment of today; a true understanding of where risks may affect the certainty of project success is required at this early stage.

Environmental assessment

In selecting options for further study, effects on the environment must always be considered in practice. The preliminary appraisal should define the likely effects of each option, to highlight potential problems such as pollution and to check if the surrounding area affected by the option is subject to any special contraints.

Social assessment

If a project may affect a community socially, the advantages and disadvantages to that community need due consideration. In developing countries, the effects on the local population of a new project can be particularly severe.

At this stage, the implications of each option for the people affected directly and indirectly should be explored. Two rather obvious examples are the creation of jobs (a social as well as an economic factor) and the displacement and resettlement of communities affected by land take.

Practical considerations

A project that may seem an attractive proposition on paper might nevertheless run into problems of acceptance by the planning authorities, for example. In many instances in the UK, planning permission is required where change of land use and new developments are concerned, and there could also be the prospect of a Public Inquiry. There is little use in proceeding with project preparation if the scheme stands no chance of obtaining permission. The procedures should be understood and their effects on the project considered, particularly with regard to the timetable for development. The investigations at this stage must therefore include assessment of these aspects, to be taken into account in risk analysis (see section 3.8).

3.7 Overall appraisal and recommendations

During the appraisal it is usually easier to keep the details of the various aspects separate, except of course for basic interlinks — for example, an investment plan cannot be produced without a project planning input. The analysis having been completed, it is a fairly simple task to weigh up all the factors and decide which options should be included in the feasibility studies.

The fresh information assembled during the preliminary appraisal may place the original aims in a new light; the objectives should therefore be discussed with the Client and confirmed before the list of options is finalised.

If the results of the preliminary analysis show that the options do not meet the confirmed objectives, either the objectives or the project may have to be reconsidered. Assuming, however, that one or more of the options will achieve the aims, the comparative merits of each are listed and a tentative ranking order established. One more task is required before reaching a decision — risk analysis.

The output of this phase should include not only the list of options carried forward, but also the 'ground rules' for the feasibility stage: boundaries and limitations of the study, evaluation criteria and a tentative assessment framework (see section 4.7).

3.8 Risk analysis

To plan, design and construct a capital project successfully depends on identifying and managing risk. For example, the risk that materials or workmanship may at some point be substandard is managed in various ways, such as making allowances in the design, using quality assurance (QA) procedures, and devoting resources to quality control at site.

To give another example, the Contractor takes into account the risk that his detailed cost estimates at tender stage may be based on incomplete information or subject to a margin of error, say ± 5%, and finds ways to manage that. At higher level than all of this is the overall financial out-turn of the whole project. At every stage the risks inherent in the remaining work must be evaluated by those concerned. Success depends on assessing the risks, taking action to reduce them where practicable, and sharing as fairly as possible the cost of offsetting the remaining part.

Risk analysis during project identification has the following aims:

- to identify and to ensure awareness of the various risks that could affect the cost and timing of the project, and to recognise the alternative strategies for project implementation
- to reflect the risks associated with the project in the form of contingency allowances.

The process of identifying areas of risk and of quantifying these where possible is a thread running through the whole of this phase: staff and advisers experienced in such problems will have their assessments ready as part of the overall appraisal. However, the assessment of many areas of risk involves subjective or qualitative judgement which will at least require input from the Client himself, or in the end may rest solely on his opinion. Thus, the significance of risk analysis emerges from a dialogue or discussion that often takes place when the results of the appraisal are on the table.

Figure 3.3 demonstrates how the ability to control and influence actions decreases as the project progresses through its phases. While the Client faces the highest levels of uncertainty regarding the possible outcome of the project during the identification phase, he also has an opportunity to amend his project's strategy, process and objectives.

To take advantage of this opportunity, the Client must be aware of the potential risks associated with the undertaking. Risk analysis techniques assist him to conduct his evaluation and hence to make execution plans and strategies to avoid or alleviate risk to the overall project.

The other aim of risk analysis is to produce for each phase cost and time estimates which equal the performance that will be achieved if the project is completed. The risk is usually represented as a contingency allowance: as the project progresses the level of uncertainty decreases; this should be reflected by a reduction in the contingency allowance.

If potential project risks are assessed adequately at this stage, the escalation of project costs and slippage of the completion dates which tend to occur can be predicted and allowed for. Each of the options will carry different risks; a decision to progress one rather than another should take this variation into account.

During this phase, the deterministic data, preliminary cost estimates and programmes which may be available are themselves based on highly subjective assumptions. While an assessment should be produced, as far as possible, of all the project risks in the form of cost and time contingency allowances, the emphasis should be on the identification of major risks. To this end, qualitative techniques such as influence diagrams and the discovery of levels of management confidence should be used for risk identification.

In order to evaluate the risks so identified, 'guestimates' of the implications of the risk's occurrence in terms of cost and time should be made, tabulated and included in the estimate for each option. Key variables such as escalation of materials and labour rates should also be identified, and the sensitivity of the project economics to varying these variables by $\pm 10\%$ should be documented. At this stage, the impact of choosing different locations for the project might also be examined and highlighted. Other aids to decision-making include the use of decision trees, as noted in chapter 4.

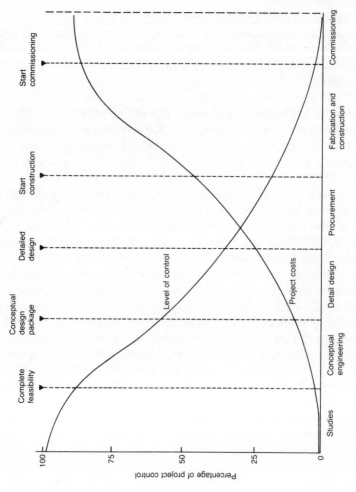

Fig. 3.3. Degree of project control

Risk analysis techniques

So far in this section we have described the place of risk analysis in the project identification phase, while keeping it in the context of subsequent continuity. Naturally, risk analysis continues throughout all phases of a project — as the quantity and accuracy of available information improves, more sophisticated methods of analysis are introduced, at least in projects sufficiently large and complex to justify their use.

These methods fall into two groups: qualitative techniques which document and assess mainly judgmental or subjective data such as those dealing with organisational, political and human relations issues; and quantitative techniques which manipulate numerical data for forecast ranges of time and cost out-turns. The use of these groups of risk analysis methods during the life of a project is shown in Fig. 3.5.

Because qualitative methods are used in situations where few or no precise measures or numbers are available, they tend to be employed more in the early stages.

Influence diagrams. This method is useful in establishing the type and seriousness of the risks involved in the planning, running and organisation of a project. An influence diagram is a map of those key project interrelationships which affect key management issues. It structures and links a variety of project factors, and highlights the type of influence of one on another.

Decision analysis. Decision tree analysis helps individuals to assess options, minimise costs for a given level of risk, and select an appropriate level of risk for a project. A decision tree consists of branches and event and decision nodes. It enables management to compute the optimum pay-off at each node and to choose the best route at each decision node; and is used, for example, in reviewing investment options and in considering the effects of project changes during implementation.

Management confidence technique (MCT). This new technique is a practical tool which considers the risks resulting from the combined effects of all constraints acting on a project. It represents a useful structured approach to identifying potential areas of risk in the project's planning or organisation. In practice, MCT requires an analysis in the form of questions about actual constraints on a project. It demands that management give a specific numbered weighting to all constraints listed against the project. Each

33

Project risk techniques	Project phases					
	Identification	Feasibility	Concept engineering	Detailed engineering	Procurement and construction	Commissioning
Quantitative						
Sensitivity analysis	XX	XXX	XX	X	O	O
Sum of maxima and minima	XX	XXX	X	O	O	O
Simulation/probabilistic techniques	X	XX	XXX	XXX	XX	X
The successive principle	O	O	XXX	XXX	O	O
Qualitative						
Influence diagrams	XXX	XX	O	O	O	O
Decision analysis	XXX	XXX	XX	XX	X	O
Management confidence technique	XXX	XX	X	O	O	O

xxx very relevant;   xx relevant;   x unusual;   O typically not used

Fig. 3.4. *Use of risk analysis techniques during project development*

constraint factor is determined by the manager; overall constraint values are calculated to show how these affect project performance. These figures are then used as a basis for comparative evaluation of the 'riskiness of options', and are presented in a graphical format.

As regards the group of quantitative techniques, the purpose of Fig. 3.4 is to show in which project phase each may become relevant. This group comprises the following.

Sensitivity analysis. The best known way of using 'what if?' questions, for example 'What will be the effect on financial viability if production costs rise/fall by 10%?'. It is easy nowadays, with the right software, to ask many such questions for each option (see chapter 4), studying changes of one variable at a time.

Sum of maxima and minima. A sensitivity evaluation method used where several variables have specified upper and lower limits, but there is no given range of intermediate probabilities.

Simulation. Mathematical models, simulation and probabilistic techniques are widely used in large complex projects. These powerful tools typically model continuous curves of probabilities related to each event (variable) by dividing the range into finite intervals, either coarsely or finely as the user requires. This simulation software uses a large amount of processor and memory capacity, and involves effort in setting up the codex and data input to the computer. These methods have been found to be especially relevant to large projects in the petrochemical and defence industries.

The successive principle. This is analogous to a decision tree, using a probabilistic method applied to event−sequence networks.

Decision analysis. This is mentioned above as a qualitative technique, but in practice the evaluator would try wherever possible to obtain numerate ranges of values, on a confidential basis if necessary.

It is worth repeating the statement at the beginning of this section that projects are concerned with the identification and management of risk. Truly, no-one wants to invent problems or to meet trouble halfway; but to say 'We'll cross that bridge when we come to it', or 'It'll be all right', is no way to carry on a business when there is a 30% chance that 'it' will go wrong and no-one has bothered to think about it. Risk analysis, whether using simple or complex methods, is essential.

3.9 Review topics

- The project identification phase comprises a preliminary appraisal of the project, with the aim of deciding whether or not the next (feasibility) phase should be undertaken and of providing selected options for study.
- A review of this phase should establish whether or not the following important factors have been satisfactorily covered in the appraisal:

  o clear statement of project objectives
  o understanding of the Client organisation
  o listing of other participants and their influence
  o determining the constraints on the project
  o determining the criteria for the appraisal
  o determining likely sources of funding
  o selection of likely options for development
  o assessment of data, data sources and data reliability
  o calculation of project profitability and benefits, with ranges of values
  o presentation of the product of this phase, including a short list of options to be considered and a framework of references for the feasibility phase.

4 Project planning and feasibility phase

4.1 Introduction

It was mentioned in chapter 1 that the feasibility study phase, although executed before the project design starts, is a significant type of project evaluation. The purpose of this chapter is to describe such a study.

The feasibility study takes as its starting point the output of the project identification phase, including clear terms of reference, the list of options, and at least some of the criteria for judging them. The study may be short or lengthy, simple or complex, depending on circumstances; in any case it is one of the principal stages in project development, and should be designed to give the Client an early assessment of the viability of the project, and the degree of risk attached.

The general term 'viability' refers to the ability of a project to meet predetermined objectives, which may be technical, economic, social, financial, or a combination of these. In turn, a project may be said to be financially or commercially viable if it meets the objectives of profitability by acceptable means; financial viability thus relates to a number of criteria in combination, including profitability, limitation of investment, restraints on cash flow, and timing.

The outcome of this phase should be the selection of a defined project which meets the stated project objectives, together with a broad plan of implementation. To this end, the studies should involve sufficiently detailed investigations to establish financial viability, the effects of environmental and social impact, and the technical and operational suitability of the project. Variations may be considered which in themselves have considerable impact on overall viability. An effective feasibility study should use consistent

37

methods and levels of detail in preliminary design and estimates of costs and benefits over all options. Several substudies are usually worked in parallel, but these are strongly interactive, as consideration of design options, time, cost and contractual strategies are all interlinked.

In this chapter a typical feasibility study is outlined in five stages. The study structure is intended to indicate aspects of a project visible to the public eye; the criteria for judgement appropriate in such a case are indicated by means of examples. Where standard procedures are laid down by the Client or other authority, they should be followed.

The first stage is devoted to planning. The study brief should be reviewed and confirmed — this is most important if there has been a break in continuity after the previous phase. A simple network of activities should be produced, in any convenient form, with time and resources estimates. In all but the simplest cases these studies tend to become overcomplicated because of their high degree of uncertainty; time and resources need management. A significant part of the effort is spent in collecting and analysing the data that will be required for evaluation. While this exercise should not be so constrained that important items are omitted, the effort can be minimised in practice. For example, a small team with the necessary experience can discuss and visualise the evaluation process, specify the form and timing of input from one activity to others dependent on it. In short, an agreed study plan should provide a firm working basis, yet should be flexible enough to accommodate the main uncertainties.

Once the study plan has been agreed, the work proceeds through the remaining four stages:

- project development
- impact appraisal
- project evaluation
- conclusions and decisions.

The sequence of stages is shown in Fig. 4.1; each is described in the following sections.

Many people are inclined to dismiss the need for feasibility studies because in hindsight their predictions are found to be erroneous. In practice, the results of a study are not immutable for all time. A well-executed study should of course give confidence to those

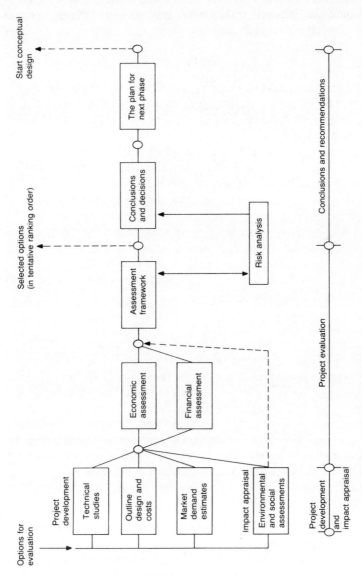

Fig. 4.1. The project feasibility stage

involved in the decisions, but it should be regarded, not as a prediction of events, but as an indication of a likely range of probabilities. The events themselves may turn out differently; hence the importance of risk analysis.

4.2 Project development
To enable appraisal of a proposed project, it must be developed to at least an outline design. Judgement is needed in assembling the necessary information while avoiding the pitfalls of too detailed an investigation.

It is usually a waste of time to produce plans or designs for each option in great detail, even if the laudable aim is to determine costs more accurately. One reason for this is that financial viability has yet to be proved; another is that most of the options will be dropped anyway. For present purposes, the watchword should be consistency in the treatment of all options, so that true comparisons can be achieved. At an appropriate level of detail, therefore, the options should be examined with regard to preliminary technical studies, outline design, demand estimates, cost estimates and planning for implementation.

Technical studies
In the present context, 'technical studies' means investigations related to the site, surroundings and services. For capital works projects, an initial visit to the site (or sites, if more than one location is still to be considered) to establish its topographical and geotechnical charactersitics is necessary. The cost of a major industrial or public utility project can depend on ground conditions — for example, large volumes of hard rock may need to be excavated or extensive piling might be required to overcome poor load bearing or poorly drained ground conditions.

Other studies which may be required to suit particular projects include the following.

- Surveys of the location and capacity of public utilities (water, drainage, electricity, gas and telecommunications), and assessment of the cost and time implications of new infrastructure developments if these are needed for the project.
- Surveys of adjacent land uses and activities, e.g. residential, industrial, commercial, and open space (for later impact

studies). Constraints such as possible existing contamination and historical importance should be considered.

- The town and country planning policy context — zoning (see section 4.3).
- Transportation and access considerations. Any new development or redevelopment is likely to affect the local road/rail network; also, the cost of any required contribution to the local Highway Authority to create the necessary additional capacity must be recognised.
- Sources and availability of construction materials and labour.

Outline design

The outline design of the project should show sufficient detail to allow technical and operational feasibility to be confirmed, global cost estimates to be given, and meaningful impact assessments to be made. For industrial projects, various types of process may be considered and preliminary material flow diagrams produced, as a basis for outline design and costing of each option.

For building-oriented projects, the example of a city centre commercial development gives a good indication of the details required:

- plot ratio and overall gross and net floor area
- on-site parking requirements
- access for service vehicles
- type of construction, internal/external materials
- standard of provision of building services
- linkage with public utility networks.

Demand estimates

Market studies to assess demand for the project were included in the previous phase. These should now be confirmed and extended to answer the following questions.

- Is there an existing or potential demand for the use or product being proposed?
- Will this demand be sustained for a sufficiently long time to fulfil the project objectives?
- Are there competing prospects; if so, are they more or less advanced?
- Does the chosen location best suit the market demand?

41

- Can a pricing policy be defined; what are the influences on prices?

The basis of the forecasts must be sufficiently robust to support the operation of the facility or the proposed product output, as the case may be, throughout the life of the project (see the typical example in Fig. 4.2). It should be noted that accuracy over long periods into the future is unlikely — the longer the project life, the wider the range of possible forecasts becomes. This affects some projects more than others, particularly with regard to such criteria as internal rate of return (see financial assessment, section 4.4). Fortunately, the early years are the most important for many small or medium-sized projects; even so, short-term forecasts should always be subjected to sensitivity analysis.

Cost estimates

Cost estimates of options under consideration should be prepared during this phase. It is worth emphasising again that these estimates must be directly comparable, even though the options being compared are dissimilar.

Typically, during this phase, the first serious effort should be made to establish a final cost for the project. This estimate is reconciled with the initial order of magnitude figures. It then becomes the basis against which cost developments in the conceptual engineering phase are compared and justified. This estimate is also used to produce cash flows of the funding requirements of the project.

Preliminary estimate of project timescales

In the eary stages of a project, the end date is often the only known milestone. Timescales are planned by breaking the project down into likely contracts or physical elements of the work. The draft project planning models should be discussed with the senior project executives, using high-level network diagrams or linked barcharts — such discussions can quickly highlight misconceptions or lack of understanding of the project objectives.

Although at this stage the engineering aspects are defined only in broad terms, it should be possible to establish planning models that can be resourced, priced and then evaluated from the point of view of cost, cash flow, and ability to meet the outline timescales.

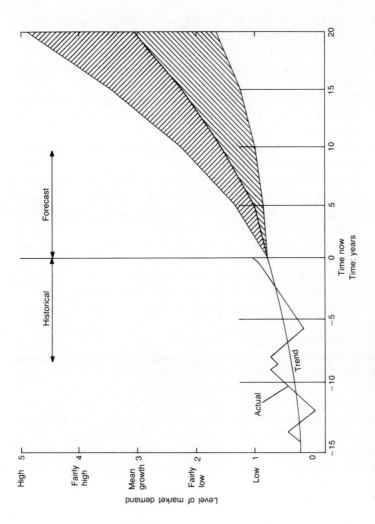

Fig. 4.2.   Range of market forecasts

To some extent, the acceptability of the models will depend on availability of data from similar projects.

The following questions should be addressed in this phase.

- Is there a plan for conducting the feasibility studies, and is it being monitored regularly?
- Have the major contract breakdowns been decided?
- Does the planning model reflect the major interactions within the project?
- Have the estimates of duration for each physical element been estabished (e.g. by factoring timescales of suitable similar projects)?
- Has an estimate of scope in terms of man-hours or cost been made for each element?
- Has a resource analysis been conducted on the project programme, and adjusted to avoid excessive peaks and troughs?
- Has the contract strategy been reflected in both the pre-contract and contract programme durations?
- Has an outline programme for the next phase (conceptual engineering) and the methods of controlling it been developed and discussed within the project team?
- Has sufficient contingency been included and allocated in the programme for delays and any probable technical set-backs?

4.3 Impact appraisal

In the past, development projects may at times have attracted only moderate interest in the local community. In recent years, however, the involvement of special interest groups in particular and public participation in general has become more apparent.

It is now essential that the impact of the proposed development is realistically assessed, both by the developer or investor and the relevant local or central government planning body. This impact can be extensive, and an impact appraisal must consider the relevance of the following factors.

- Land use: what is the impact of the proposed project on adjacent land uses? (See *Technical studies* above.) For housing or commercial schemes, is the proposed development compatible with those adjacent to it; do the proposed residential or office floor space densities exceed local standards?
- Planning policy: does the proposed development conform to

both the zoning and local planning policy framework? Where conflicts arise, do they affect the likelihood of obtaining planning permission?

- Environmental issues: what impact will the proposed development have on the landscape and on sites of special scientific interest or nature reserves? Will any form of pollution (e.g. noise, air, water) result from it? If so, the Client should quantify it if possible and use such information in discussions with the local planning authority. Can the impact be reduced significantly by site landscaping or otherwise?

- Infrastructure: any new form of development must inevitably have an impact on transportation and public utility considerations. For example, does the local road and public utility network have sufficient capacity to absorb the proposed development? Will off-site traffice management measures be required, or will planning gain be introduced by the creation of a new road link or new sewage treatment works?

- Social and economic aspects: these affect employment, retail income in the local economy and the provision of additional community facilities. The jobs created and money earned will be retained to varying degrees in the local economy, thereby creating additional benefits.

From a technical point of view, it will be prudent for the Client to consider and be aware of all likely impacts, whether positive or negative. Some problems can be overcome at additional cost by on-site landscaping and screening, or by the provision of additional pollution control, infrastructure or community benefits. The immediate use for the results of the environmental and social assessments is in project evaluation, when the Client can assess the overall balance between the scheme development and impact appraisal analysis in order to decide whether to proceed with the project or abandon it.

4.4 Project evaluation

Reference was made in the previous section to 'the first serious attempt to establish a final cost'. A large part of the present evaluation is comparative: considering and applying weighting to the criteria so as to place the options in order of acceptability (see section 4.5). However, the feasibility study must also produce a statement of the financial viability of the top-ranking options. Although we are only at the feasibility stage, a decision to proceed will involve real expenditure on engineering work — hence the importance of a reasonably accurate forecast of viability.

The evaluation process should be considered in terms of economic and financial assessment: technical, environmental and social appraisal; operational considerations, and finally the impact of variations.

Economic assessment

The economic assessment is concerned with the worth of the project to the community as well as to the developer or user (see section 3.6). The worth to the community is measured as the net resource cost savings (or benefits) deriving from the project. The topic is treated generally in this section; further details, including definitions, are given in appendix A.

The project's capital, maintenance and operating costs should be calculated in constant price terms, throughout an assumed lifetime of the project, thus producing a profile of costs against time, which is compared with the equivalent time stream of resource cost benefits. The lifetime of the project is frequently 20–30 years for infrastructure projects.

The economic assessment of a project is different and separate from the financial assessment. This distinction is best shown by considering public sector projects, such as road schemes, which do not generate a cash income to enable a direct financial assessment to be made in terms of profitability. Such schemes do, however, provide benefits in other ways which can be assessed. (Some of these potential benefits are listed below).

Two points of difference between economic and the financial assessments must be stressed.

- The two measures do not always give the same indication of project viability. The road schemes mentioned above may generate substantial economic benefit for which no direct charge is made to the user. Similarly, a project might be justified on social benefit grounds although its cost cannot realistically be recovered by charges that users can reaonably be expected to afford, for example water supply schemes to low income areas, or a rural bus service. Again, benefits to non-users of a project may be sufficient to justify its adoption in socio-economic terms even though charges to users are insufficient to ensure its financial viability: this situation has arisen in the introduction of public transport services in heavily congested urban areas, notably in developing countries.

- In contrast to the economic assessment, where all costs and benefits are expressed in resource cost terms — their financial or market values being adjusted to reflect the true cost to the economy — the financial evaluation is conducted solely in monetary terms.

The principles and methods of economic assessment can be applied to both public and private sector projects. The types of benefits which should be taken into account can be listed as follows, using a road scheme as an example:

- savings in materials and energy
- savings in time
- savings in accidents/damage etc.
- improved health and welfare
- improved productivity
- generated agricultural and industrial output
- changes in land use and land values etc.
- reduction of waste.

Care is always needed to avoid double counting, which could easily distort the calculations. The list is in no particular order, and the relative significance of the benefits varies with the nature of the project.

The net resource cost benefits are the difference between the two streams (the costs and the benefits) referred to above. The various techniques used in making the comparison are nearly always based on discounted cash flow (DCF) methods. The results of the economic assessment can be espressed in various forms, but should at least include the following for each option.

- The DCF display of net cost benefits, brought to a *net present value* (NPV) by an accepted method. The methods used or discount rates suggested by official bodies should be noted, for example, the test discount rate recommended by the UK Treasury for public works.

- Other, supplementary, indicators where appropriate — e.g. payback period.
- The DCF display of net costs showing the options with least net present cost (NPC). There should be appropriate comment as to why the option with the lowest NPC is or is not preferred.
- Need for ancillary investment, outside the project, to enable its benefit to be realised.
- Sensitivity analysis to show how the return from the project would respond to changes in basic assumptions and parameters.

Clearly, investigations of the kind required to produce these results can be lengthy and complex. Care should be taken to draw up and agree the basic assumptions and the boundaries to enable effective and useful results to be produced.

Finally, if the analysis is favourable and the project proved worthwhile, analysis using the same techniques will be required to optimise timing and phasing in relation to the benefits to be achieved.

Financial assessment

As shown above, financial evaluation is separate from economic assessment, being concerned with the return on the capital to be invested in the project. Various criteria of financial viability can be used. Some investors still tend to employ yardsticks such as the return on investment (ROI) during a year of full operation coupled with the payback period — these measures have their uses. In most cases however, and particularly in the feasibility phase, the use of DCF techniques is required and will enable a more accurate estimate of the out-turn, as well as a better standard of risk assessment.

The basis of the evaluation is a comparison of project capital and operating and maintenance costs with the revenues accruing to the project. The latter are derived from product sales, use of facilities and provision of services. The comparison should be made in constant price terms, and should extend throughout the service life of the project.

The evaluation period, as in the case of economic assessment, is frequently 20–30 years for infrastructure projects, but for most other works time horizons tend to be shorter. The difference between revenue flow and cost flow, year by year, gives the timestream of net cash flows. Using DCF techniques, the commercial viability of the project is measured by its internal rate of return (IRR) in real terms before consideration of financing costs and the effects of inflation. The value of the IRR is the annual discount rate which when applied to the annual net cash flow stream yields an NPV of zero (see appendix A). In the same analysis the end of payback period can be identified as the year in which the accumulated cash flow in real terms becomes positive.

The IRR can be strongly dependent on the presumed lifespan of the project, notably where the cash flow profile becomes positive relatively late in the evaluation period, or where it is likely to show progressive growth in the future. For this reason, it is important that sensitivity analysis includes consideration of this variable.

Sensitivity analysis of the results should also be made, to test the effects of changes in such other variables as cost levels, pricing or tariff structures, revenues, and timing and phasing of development. The analysis will indicate the commercial robustness of the scheme.

So far, the evaluation should be conducted in *constant price terms*, but the future flows of costs and revenues will be subject to inflation, hence a further calculation of cash flow profiles must be made to include the effects of inflation. These cash flows are said to be expressed in *money* or *current price terms*. Alternative forecast rates of inflation and levels of interest rates can be tested to show the effect on payback period and other aspects such as project funding.

Further assessment designed to explore other financial implications would include: statements on the source and application of funds; analysis of liquidity and profitability ratios; and impact of operating (as well as capital) costs. While the capital costs are always a significant factor, the choice between options is often dictated by the impact of operating costs. This has long been recognised in the industrial field, but is now also applied to building projects. Increased costs, particularly of mechanical and electrical services, as well as the advent of the 'throwaway' building, created the need to choose between high cost long-life materials and cheaper materials of shorter life. The process by which capital projects are assessed on the basis of considering all the relevant economic impacts of proceeding is known as life cycle costing or cost in use (some notes on this subject are given in appendix C).

49

A comparative life cycle costing for the best few options ought in most cases to be made at this stage.

The estimates of operating costs are usually based on historical or published data and the assessments of in-house operators. It is worth mentioning again that a detailed build-up of capital and operating costs is inappropriate because of the inaccuracies of the base assumptions.

The description of complex financial requirements and methods given in this section may seem strange to many people concerned with more straightforward commercial building developments. Frequently in such situations a minimum acceptable level of ROI is specified with a short payback period; the revenue can be predicted from knowledge of the property market and the cost of the building itself is fairly accurately known from historical data — the principal variable may well be site development costs. Thus, the availability of relevant reliable data shortens the financial assessment considerably and reflects a different set of assumptions as the starting point. The attention of the developer is focused more on the funding and on decisions such as when and how the disposal of the building will be arranged.

Assessment frameworks

At this point, an economic assessment, a financial assessment and an impact appraisal have been made for each of the options. The various factors and criteria should then be considered together in an overall evaluation (see Fig. 4.1). If the evaluation is complicated, an assessment framework may be useful. This is a form of social accounting or planning balance sheet, in which all costs, benefits and impacts can be assembled. Its aim is to identify and assist in balancing the various, sometimes conflicting, assessments and their implications for Client, user and non-user groups. It is a tool for use in, but does not replace, the decision-making process.

The framework can be in any convenient form. For example, a matrix on paper may be used, showing costs and benefits and any links between them, or the framework can comprise a simple check list of criteria, repeated for each option. However the contents are presented, they should be relevant, meaningful and consistent.

The assessments and impacts to be displayed depend on the project, but may include:

- the various forms of economic benefit
- details of the findings of the financial analysis
- capital, operating and maintenance costs
- EC and other special status grants or tax benefits
- implications for supplementary and ancilliary investment
- implications of changes in land use
- implications for supply industries
- changes in the value of land — increased value of output, change in agricultural use etc.
- value of land reclamation
- value of avoidance of agricultural and urban land/property damage
- impact on cost of urban development/infrastructure provision
- impact on planning policy, including planning gain through the freeing of land elsewhere from development pressures
- impact on employment and income creation
- social impact and repercussion
- implications of material and equipment supply
- environmental impact
- implications for conservation policy, amenity and safety etc.

Many project costs and benefits can be quantified in monetary terms and the framework can incorporate the findings of the economic analysis (NPV, NPC, IRR etc.) and financial appraisal (costs, commercial returns, cash flow implications, funding issues etc.) in this way. Risk and sensitivity can be similarly shown.

Such other issues as operational efficiency, social, environmental, conservation, amenity and safety aspects, and land use/landscape may not always be measurable in monetary terms. It may be possible to show the impact of such factors in other units, for example number of jobs created, number of properties affected, land areas affected, noise decibel levels, particle levels in air pollution, and measures of water contamination. In cases where no such measure is practicable, impacts should be described in qualitative terms using a generally accepted and limited vocabulary.

The conclusions from the assessments shown by the framework will be reached by combining two types of action:

- taking the entire matrix and identifying the nature and scale of each element and how the various interested parties are

affected — balance sheets can be assembled to identify the gainers and losers
- application of a weighting system — alternative systems can be applied to the matrix to reflect different development priorities or objectives, or to reflect different user interests. In this process, and indeed in the assessment of less quantifiable impacts, it is useful to know what weighting the community attaches to the various factors.

The end product of the assessment framework comprises:

- a statement of costs and benefits
- a clear understanding of the nature of each individual impact, positive and negative
- an understanding of the manner in which each interested party is affected.

As a result, appraisal of the scheme or selection from alternatives can be conducted with a full understanding of the implications and inherent 'trade-offs'.

4.5 Risk analysis

Chapter 3 included an outline of risk analysis techniques and their applicability at the various stages of project development. At this stage, near the end of the feasibility studies, project evaluation is concerned with the combined results of those studies, the review of the reliability of data and the assumptions involved, and the areas of uncertainty to be taken into account.

The purpose of applying risk management and analysis in this phase is to provide management with a clearer insight as to:

- what major sources of risk(s) must be taken into account
- what decisions must be made between alternative project schemes
- whether or not the project can be economically justified
- what levels of financing are required for the project.

The use of risk analysis should assist the Client in understanding the risks that emerge from any estimates or cash flows produced and in applying realistic contingencies.

One of the most valuable tools is sensitivity analysis, which can be applied to the numerate (i.e. quantifiable) results for each option so as to yield a measure of their relative robustness under changing conditions. The following example illustrates how the analysis may proceed for a factory project.

Step 1. List the parameters that may be subject to change and rework the cash flow calculations, taking specific degrees of change from the 'best assessment' situation.

Increase/decrease in (item)	Degree of change	Effect on		
		NPV	IRR	Payback
Sales opportunity (volume)	± 10%			
Sale price of products	± 10%			
Unit cost of materials	± 10%			
Labour costs	± 15%			
Funding interest rate	± 5%			
Capital cost	± 10%			
Delay in commissioning	1 year			
Delay in achieving full production	6 months			

In each calculation only one variable is changed; the rest are kept constant.

Step 2. Calculate the effects of combined variables. Because in the mathematical sense the output results represent continuous functions, the above table serves as a ready reckoner from which the effects of various percentage changes in several variables combined can be ascertained.

In using this analysis, judgement is needed to assess the probability that a particular combination will occur, and to decide whether or not is should be considered. Each option under review will be subject to different risks in respect of at least some variables, and the overall effects of these differences can alter the ranking order in which the options were previously placed.

Step 3. Consider other, indirect effects. About half the criteria discussed in section 4.4 (*Assessment frameworks*) are qualitative in character; the risks associated with them are matters of judgement.

Some types of risk may be reduced to simply allowing a sum

of money for solving the problem: as a basic example, suppose that a factory project may not be environmentally acceptable unless noise and visual intrusion are minimised by landscaping or equivalent treatment — this is then a risk that can be covered by a contingency allowance. Other types of risk may, however, be more ineluctable and capable of resolution only after further enquiry.

Thus, the risk analysis should wherever possible produce contingency allowances in terms of cost and time for each option considered. These contingencies are sometimes significant: allowances of 45% of the estimated capital cost are not uncommon at the concept stage for complex petrochemical or marine projects.

4.6 Conclusions of the feasibility study

The results of the overall evaluation should enable the Client to decide with considerable confidence whether or not the project is feasible and worth pursuing. If we assume that a preferred option has emerged, i.e. an option that displays an acceptable level of economic and financial viability and in general best fulfils the aims of the project, the decision to proceed on that basis is a likely outcome. The next step would be to redefine the aims and scope of the project, if necessary, to take account of modifications which may have appeared during the feasibility studies.

It is important that this redefinition be formalised before the end of the feasibility phase, so that any loose ends are tied in and a firm basis is provided for the next phase (conceptual engineering). In some projects, further consultations may be required, for example with a Local Authority to resolve outstanding issues or to progress a planning application. Thus, the feasibility phase should not be regarded as ending when the project evaluation is presented to the Client.

The completion of the evaluation and the decision to proceed further with the project is a significant milestone in the development. The quality of assessment will be reflected in the quality of the decisions — where, in past cases, the quality has turned out to be dubious some of the reasons have been only too clear, for example:

- poor analysis of information or over-optimistic predictions, both of which can result in bad decisions

- inadequate cost evaluation
- an inflexible approach, using only preconceived established methods in assessing project strategy
- lack of commitment by some project personnel
- lack of emphasis on organisational aspects and control.

The conclusions and decisions arising from the study should be incorporated in a project plan, as described below.

4.7 Planning of details and implementation

The final task of the feasibility phase should be the preparation of the project plan, covering the design and implementation of the project. The plans should take account of the interaction between design, operation, construction and contractual issues, and should include the following features:

- a summary of the project, its main physical characteristics and its historical background
- a statement of the Client's objectives; priorities with respect to time, cost and quality; and philosophy towards achieving the objectives
- further refinement of the selected technical design or option
- criteria and terms of reference for conceptual engineering
- chart of the basic project organisation
- roles and responsibilities of the participants; relationships and communications
- development of risk analysis and contingency allowances
- establishment of basic contractual strategy, maintaining flexibility where required
- refinement of cost estimates and establishment of overall budgets with suitable contingencies
- establishment of the basic schedule for the project with the detailed planning of the next phase
- outline work breakdown structures for the detailed design phase
- planning of liaison with external bodies, including statutory undertakings
- a detailed financial plan, including refined cash flow predictions, financial strategy, financial appraisal and funding conditions

- confirmation of the basic operating philosophy; detailing of operating costs.

The establishment of an overall project plan concludes the activities required for the project planning and feasibility stage.

4.8 Review topics

The feasibility study should be designed to produce:

- assessment of viability
- assessment of risks
- a broad plan for project implementation.

A review of the feasibility phase should establish whether or not the following significant features have been satisfactorily covered in the study:

- analysis of each option in respect of technical studies, outline design, demand estimates (for products or facilities), costs, planning and economics
- comparative and consistent analysis of all options
- impact appraisal in environmental, social and planning terms
- risk analysis and risk management
- consultations with external authorites
- production of the plan for project implementation (as outlined in section 4.7).

5 Conceptual engineering phase

5.1 Introduction

The conceptual engineering phase builds on the results of the feasibility study and is the last phase of the internal planning process. Alternative options fade into the background; the project team has its sights firmly set on discovering the best ways of bringing the chosen scheme to reality. In this chapter conceptual engineering is described, with the aim of identifying the questions that an evaluation of this phase should take into consideration. Such a review might well be made, for example, at the end of this phase, when the project is seen for the first time with all engineering problems solved, at least in outline, and cost budgets defined.

The central activity is the creation of the design concept in sufficient detail to provide a firm basis for detailed design and engineering. This process must of necessity limit the flexibility that would allow alterations late in the basic design. As a general rule, this phase provides the last chance for the Client to alter the concept or scope radically without exposing the project to the probability of considerable delays and extra costs. At the end of this phase, in most cases, the Client makes the major commitment to external consultants or contractors that in turn marks the beginning of greatly accelerated growth in the rate of investment — sometimes called the exponential growth phase — as was seen in Fig. 3.3.

The S-curve (rate of investment) is shown again in Fig. 5.1, as a measure of the size of the project organisation and the way in which the deployment of manpower and materials increases as the development progresses. Below the S-curve, Fig. 5.1 shows the degree of involvement and control exercised by the Client, the designers and the contractors in each phase. In the conceptual

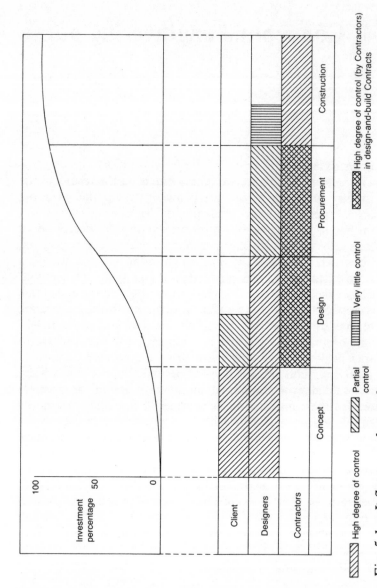

Fig. 5.1. Influence and control

engineering phase the influence at first rests with the Client and designers; as the work proceeds the prime influence passes to the designers, and finally the execution of construction is in the hands of the contractors. This is a normal contract pattern.

Alternatively in a design-and-build contract situation the product of conceptual engineering is a performance specification ('avant-projet') and the Contractor's influence on the details of the work is confined mainly to the early stages. Attempts to impose direct influence later on (except in a few specialised aspects) are fraught with difficulty, because the Client is too far from the massive array of details, and too much effort is required to master them sufficiently to control the effects of changes made. It would be disingenuous to say that the Client has no control over the details of cost and time during construction — the Client is the paymaster and may make changes to the project at any time, but once contractual commitments have been made, it becomes much more difficult to make changes without incurring delays and extra costs.

The aims of the conceptual engineering phase are best described in terms of the output normally expected from it. First, in technical terms the selected option should be refined and detailed, taking account of the latest performance standards and cost criteria and thus setting a firm basis for the following phases of detailed design. Preparation of performance and requirement specifications are an intrinsic part of this process, the subject of section 5.2.

Second, the project execution plan produced in the feasibility phase should be reviewed and amplified to provide an effective guide for the remainder of the project. The revised plan should incorporate all new information being generated, including both the design and such other elements as cost and time budget plans, cash flow requirements, resources schedules and control systems. These issues are discussed in section 5.3.

The use of the term 'project management' rather than 'project plan' as the heading for section 5.3 underlines the need for project management to be active from the start of this phase. The need for a project plan can hardly be denied; it follows that the project manager should be seen to be responsible for setting up the plan and organising the project in such a way that the conceptual design responds to well-defined and clear objectives, properly communicated. Time devoted to planning at this juncture is not wasted; it should obviate difficulties at later stages.

Reviews of projects that have failed in the past show lack of a detailed plan and of a project manager (as defined in chapter 2) appointed at this stage to be common causes of poor project performance.

5.2 Conceptual design

The first step in the conceptual design should be to optimise the design in accordance with the Client's requirements and priorities; the layouts and principal dimensions should then be established and the performance criteria defined.

If the detailed design is to be undertaken by organisations which are not involved in the conceptual design, the work of each should be defined. The drawings, schedules and other information that will comprise the product of the conceptual design must be produced in a form that enables each work package to be identified. This boundary marks a formal break between the two design phases — it may not be so clearly visible, however, where the conceptual and detailed design are within the scope of one organisation.

The design organisation

The design organisation is determined by technical factors and by the Client's policy for project implementation. In deciding how the design function should be packaged, established patterns for the industry concerned should preferably be followed, unless there is a real advantage in changing to meet the particular needs of the project. This course is advantageous in that the parties have a clear understanding of their obligations, responsibilities and relationships to one another.

Other technical factors to be considered include, first, that the nature of the technology concerned may show that a split between conceptual and detailed engineering, or between design and construction, is impracticable. Second, there may be only a few organisations available that are capable of carrying out the design. Third, for projects requiring a range of specialised engineering inputs, there may be a choice between discrete design organisations and one with a multidisciplinary capability. The use of separate organisations has the advantage that the Client can select those perceived to offer the best capability in each technology. However, the selection process is influenced by price competition, and many

Client organisations are so structured that cost factors may outweigh technical preference.

Splitting up the design work can often leave open the question of how and by whom the separate organisations will be co-ordinated. Conversely, the appointment of a single firm with a wide range of technical skills to do all the design has the advantage of unified responsibility for design and co-ordination. This benefit should, of course, be considered in relation to any weaknesses in the firm with respect to certain technologies and their application to the particular project. Thus, there are no definite rules; each case should be decided according to the circumstances.

Design optimisation

Every design is a compromise between requirements that may be in mutual conflict or that cannot all be satisfied at the same time. These include product mix, technology, material flows, matching of plant items, space, layout, traffic circulation, safety, capital cost, operating cost and programme as well as the quality of the design. The conceptual design should strike the best balance between requirements — striking this balance is an interactive process called design optimisation.

The performance criteria governing the optimisation should be defined beforehand, usually in the project plan. Both the size and the priority of each requirement should be specified, so as to show, for example, which criteria are the most important ones to which others must yield in the case of a conflict. If the criteria are not clear, an experienced design team will usually submit their own proposals to fill the gaps, and obtain the Client's approval before starting the design.

The process of optimisation can be illustrated with reference to the Channel Tunnel project. This is a rapid rail transit system which will use special rolling stock (shuttles) to carry road vehicles and must also accommodate through passenger and freight trains from the national rail networks. The equipment must therefore be compatible with the needs of users having different operating objectives and rolling stock. In the design, factors such as speed, aerodynamic drag and tunnel diameter will interact and affect the performance of the shuttles and hence the whole system. Small increases in drag have a large effect on electrical power consumption, which in turn affects the cooling loads. Complex ventilation systems and stringent safety requirements affect the design; signalling, operating systems and terminal layouts all influence the performance.

A logical sequence of optimisation should first establish performance criteria, such as the types and numbers of vehicles to be carried and the transit speeds. All the design specialists — rolling stock designers, manufacturers, aerodynamicists, service engineers — should then be involved in determining the dimensions of the shuttle trains; hence, the required tunnel diameter can be calculated. This process requires many iterations, as well as research into some aspects, before an acceptable balance of systems, performance, capital and operating cost is achieved. Naturally, any delay in the optimisation process has an immediate effect on the construction programme.

In parallel with tunnel design, the layouts and approach roads at the terminals are optimised to suit the predicted traffic throughput, on the basis of the outline planning studies made previously, in the feasibility stage. While the Channel Tunnel project is rare in terms of the concept and the binational organsiation, the complexity and interdependence of its operational and technological requirements are by no means unusual. Thus, the foregoing example emphasises that the optimisation stage should be based on planning and co-ordination of the activities, appropriate to the complexity anticipated in the design. A review of this process should consider whether or not the following features received sufficient attention:

- a clear and concise brief which defines the design performance objectives and priorities
- a plan which is sequenced and allows for iteration to enable optimisation of the design with inputs from all technical specialisations
- the active involvement of the Client and/or the user
- good communications between and within all design organisations
- timely availability of specialist data, e.g. selected studies, geotechnical investigations, market research
- quality assurance policy and procedures
- close liaison between design and the cost and planning activities so that the cost and time implications of various solutions can be evaluated as the design evolves

- good reporting, which gives balanced reviews of the various solutions under consideration.

Design packaging

The breakdown of the detailed design into work packages should be decided in preparation for the next phase. The design organisations should also contribute to the contract strategy, to which the scheduling and allocation of design tasks must be tailored. The degree of definition depends on whether the detailed design is to be performed by those undertaking the conceptual design, is to be open to negotiated or competitive selection, or is to form part of a design-and-construct contract. If the project is to be built to a tight programme, it may be necessary to consider an overlap between design and construction phases.

However the design is packaged, the terms of reference for each package should cover the following:

- a clear definition of interfaces between design organisations; responsibilities defined so as to facilitate management of such interfaces
- integration with chosen contract strategy
- availability of design deliverables to suit the project programme
- standards and regulations to be followed
- timely definition of long lead procurement
- flexibility to accommodate changes where required.

Note that a 'design deliverable' is a set of drawings, documents or other information required to be produced by a given date and so specified in the relevant design contracts.

Design interfaces

Design interfaces can be defined as boundaries where design tasks meet or overlap; they can exist between design organisations, between technical specialisations and between design packages. Project management should be concerned with these and with interfaces between those responsible for cost, programme, procurement, safety, construction, commissioning, operations and maintenance.

The avoidance of loose co-ordination and the need for the management of design interfaces are emphasised above. The purpose is not just to make things fit together and thus avoid expensive redesign or reconstruction, but to ensure that individual elements work well together as a whole, and that they are economical to construct and easy to maintain.

The project manager should ensure that the management and technical problems outlined above are resolved, and in doing so would at least expect:

- involvement of all design disciplines early in this phase
- common awareness of design interfaces as a potential problem
- regular co-ordination meetings of those concerned
- use of interface drawings, agreed common boundaries on drawings, etc.
- planning and scheduling of exchanges of information across the interfaces, related to the overall design programme.

Design planning

Planning and time scheduling of the detailed design should be conducted, keeping the design packaging and optimisation in view. The planning should be based on best estimates of the numbers of drawings and specifications to be produced and the manpower resources needed. The programme should include specified milestones and the corresponding deliverables, and should allow time for Client and third party approvals. Inputs from the Client or other organisations during the detailed design should be defined with a realistic float between estimated and contractual dates for their provision. For complex projects a network analysis may be required.

If a number of separate design organisations are to be involved throughout the design, the preparation of separate plans almost invariably results because each body has its own commercial objectives. Strong, independent project management is needed to achieve proper planning integration. Alternatively, on most design-led projects a 'lead discipline' is nominated, depending on the nature of the end product, and is usually expected to produce an overall programme and manage the technical co-ordination.

However, fully integrated planning, taking account of the requirements of all designers, is seldom seen in these situations. The use of a single design organisation with multidisciplinary capability has the advantage of unified responsibility in this area, as mentioned above. Should this option be chosen, the single design organisation should openly demonstrate that its design management is impartial, not favouring one technical specialisation at the expense of the others involved.

5.3 Project management
Aims of project management in conceptual engineering

The need for project management at this stage was raised in section 5.1; the following paragraphs enlarge on the observations made there.

Most engineers — and most clients — have a lively appreciation of the need for overall management of project execution as an identifiable activity separate from planning, design, contruction, accounting and the rest. Nevertheless, in far too many projects there is no effective overall project management, although the participants are competently managing affairs within their own scope of responsibility. In such cases, and unless the interfaces are very simple and well understood, it is unlikely that the conceptual engineering phase will have been well co-ordinated or that an effective system for the control of the detailed design and construction phases will have been established.

The project manager should be appointed by the start of the conceptual engineering phase. The person should have participated in the preparation of the project execution plan, and should be addressing the problem of deciding the means by which later stages of the project will be managed.

An effective project organisation should be established that binds all the project participants together, has short lines of communication, and collates and disseminates data efficiently. To be effective, the project manager must have delegated authority to make decisions regarding time and cost management and to formulate contract and procurement strategy. As this phase is concerned with defining the performance criteria, management should be closely involved in the design process. This involvement will be reduced to a monitoring role in later stages, when the designers must be left to design. Also, the management of the participant organisations should be finalised and computer systems and project procedures put in place.

In short, the aim of project management is to plan for future phases of the project in terms of design, procurement, management organisations, time and resource scheduling, and cost management.

Procurement strategy

During the conceptual engineering phase, procurement strategy should be refined and a detailed procurement plan established. The term 'procurement' relates to all the goods and services required for the project, and includes consideration of the construction contracts as well as the supply of the equipment and materials to be installed. Details of purchasing (supply) systems and procedures are discussed in chapter 7.

The procurement strategy should define the aims, criteria and constraints in relation to at least the following items:

- supplies required to be separated from the construction, either for early ordering (long lead) or because of client policy
- types of contract best suited to the project works or parts of them
- division of work scope between detailed design, supply, construction and commissioning; division of work into packages
- principal suppliers of main items of equipment and materials; scope of supply and delivery periods
- scope and types of subcontracts
- standard and special conditions of contract
- evaluation of available contracting resources, including prequalification of suppliers and contractors (if needed at this stage)
- outline procedures for enquiry, tender, evaluation and placing of orders.

Each item in the above list should be expanded and investigated in detail to suit the scope of the particular project. Much depends upon the question of supplies that are separated from the construction contracts; for example if many items of equipment and materials are not available in the country where the project is to be constructed. Matters that should be investigated early and settled at this stage in the procurement plan include:

- conditions of purchase
- political constraints, e.g. unacceptability of certain countries/ firms
- special tender and ordering procedures
- foreign currency constraints

- ordering procedure for bulk items — they may be ordered singly or in consignments, or a 'blanket order' may be used whereby commercial conditions are agreed but only notional quantities are given and a series of suborders are placed when appropriate
- specified suppliers — for example, some equipment may be required by the client to match existing plant, and will be procured by negotiation as opposed to competitive tender
- inspection and certification
- forwarding, shipping and insurance — whether the vendor or an agent will be responsible
- appointment of a clearing agent
- procedures for material control at site — whether materials are delivered and kept in a central store or issued directly to the construction contractors.

Most of the above points are also applicable wherever supply of equipment is separated from the construction contract. Frequently a coding system is used in equipment lists to show exactly for each item whether the supplier, the construction contractor or someone else is responsible for:

- obtaining tenders
- approval
- ordering
- supply
- delivery
- inspection
- installation at site
- testing and commissioning.

On many projects it will be decided to make all supplies the responsibility of the construction Contractor, in order to achieve unified responsibility or for other reasons. Placing the procurement responsibility with the Contractor simplifies the contractual interfaces, but some loss of control over the selection of equipment and materials is inevitable

For many industrial projects items of equipment selected from different sources have to be matched for performance, often specified by model number, integrated into the layout and material flow pattern and serviced. Consultation with the suppliers takes place at quite an early stage. The conceptual and detailed design phases are fused together; the design process does not have a clean break point until the final equipment list and specification have been produced. This can be a governing factor in choosing the procurement strategy.

All of these points are interrelated with the time scheduling and the conceptual design itself. Once the procurement strategy has been evolved the procurement plan should be written, and will consist largely of the answers to all the above items, expressed in logical form and sequence. In some cases, preparing the plan is not simply a desk exercise, but may involve surveys and studies of sources of materials, delivery times and basic costs — in fact all aspects of 'the market-place'. Where the construction site of a large project is remote from industrial centres, some at least of these studies may have already been done in the previous phase because of their effects on overall feasibility.

Lack of material is a major cause of disruption during the construction phase, and can result in delays, additional costs and the substitution of materials and equipment selected on the basis of availability rather than fitness for purpose. All too often when such a situation is examined later, its roots will be traced to the fact that there was inadequate planning of procurement at the conceptual phase.

The above comment also applies to the type of construction contract. Cost, terms of payment, technical requirements and time are fundamental in selection of the right type of contract.

Figure 5.2 shows various types of contract and the relative flexibility they afford the Client to accommodate change in a controlled manner. Fig. 5.2(a) relates to the whole range of construction contracts (with or without design work); Fig. 2(b) to management contracting arrangements. In both cases, contract types towards the lower, right-hand, part of the diagram offer greater flexibility than those near the top. Turnkey contracts are the least flexible, while cost plus types are generally regarded as appropriate where the design scope of work is likely to change during the course of the contract. The choice of contract type thus depends on the extent of change anticipated by the Client and the designers. Another factor in the choice is which project risks the Client prefers or has resources to control, and which risks should be controlled by others (the Contractor, for example).

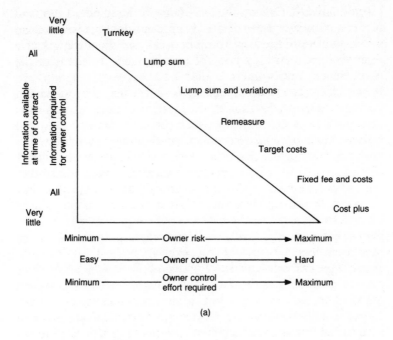

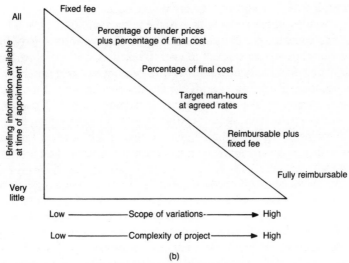

Fig. 5.2. Flexibility of various types of contracts: (a) choice of type of Contract; (b) choice of type of fee agreement

For many UK projects the use of one of the standard forms of contract is entirely appropriate. Their conditions are well known and have been refined over a period of time. In the event of a disagreement, there is a body of case law and precedent to call upon which assists interpretation of the contract conditions. However, many projects require a broader view of procurement planning during the conceptual design stage; the following discussion is in the context of such project situations.

By far the most common reason for adopting a particular form of contract is the fact that it has been used before and is familiar to the participants, who are reluctant to change. Such preconceptions usually come from the Client, although retained professional firms may also have preferences for certain types of contract. Project control procedures and the whole system of project management may be geared to a particular form of contract, which tends to be used regardless of its suitability for each application. Strategy may only change as a consequence of previous bad experiences. Often, projects go awry because of a poorly thought-out contract policy. Many examples can be cited of lump sum design-and-construct contracts let without a properly defined conceptual design, or of a 'fast track' programme adopted without a logical evaluation of complex design and construction interfaces.

The subsequent management of the project within the framework of the contract policy is just as likely to be a cause of problems as the type of contract; the two aspects should be considered together. Fig. 5.3 shows four types of contract relationships, in a situation requiring several construction contracts. The title of each example is not a precise term but merely a label for identification. Here again, flexibility is an important feature from the point of view of the Client, as also is the ease or difficulty of effective co-ordination. Each example is considered in turn below.

(a) *Management Contractor*. The Client, through his project manager, directs the design organisation in both conceptual and detailed phases, hence this arrangement is highly flexible in design. The Client has only one other organisation to direct, and his co-ordination work is relatively easy, as responsibility for managing the construction (and probably the procurement of supplies and equipment) is delegated to the Mangement Contractor. Flexibility in construction will depend on the type of contract selected.

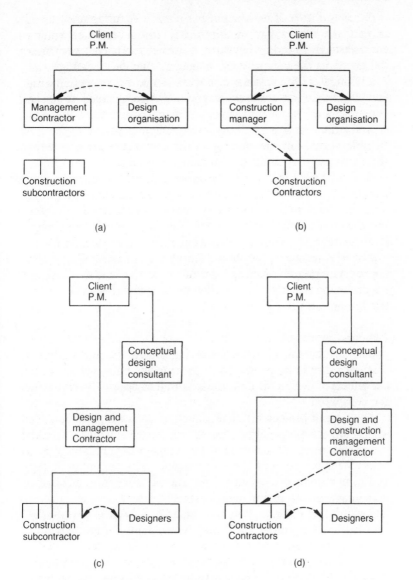

Fig. 5.3. Possible structures for the management of project contracts (a) Management Contractor; (b) Construction Management Contractor; (c) Design and Management Contractor; (d) Design and Construction Management Contractor

(b) Construction Management Contractor. The difference from (*a*) is that the Client has to administer the several construction contracts. His co-ordination work, however, is relatively easy, being delegated to the construction manager. Flexibility is high.

(c) Design and Management Contractor. Once the conceptual design is done, the Contractor takes responsibility for detailed design and construction. The Client then has only one contract to administer, so co-ordination is easy. This arrangement is probably the least flexible of the four, depending on the contract types selected. In the extreme, this could be a turnkey contract.

(d) Design and Construction Management Contractor. As in (*c*), there is a clear break between the conceptual and detailed design phases. The Client has to administer the separate construction contracts, but the co-ordination is delegated. Flexibility for design changes is lower than in (*a*) or (*b*), but probably higher than in (*c*).

The procurement plan should simplify interfaces, allow for the appropriate degree of design definition at the tender stage, and maximise the chances of completion to the specified standard within the budget and the programme.

Financial management

Early in the conceptual engineering phase, the first budget or cost plan should be produced to provide the basis against which the effects of design optimisations as well as design developments are compared.

The type of project will determine the estimating method used to develop the budget. For process or industrial facilities, factorial estimating methods are used at this stage where reliable quoted prices for major items of plant are available. The costs of bulk items and minor items of equipment are then estimated as a factor or percentage of the major plant costs.

For building projects, unit rates based on historical or published information for similar work may be available for application to the quantities required for the main items of work.

A third method occasionally used on civil engineering projects is a detailed or 'operational' estimating technique, based on an analysis of an activity resource programme and a method statement for the execution of the work. The estimate is built up from basic principles and current costs. Successful use of this method depends on availability of adequate and sufficiently detailed information.

As the work of this phase progresses, more up-to-date and detailed information is produced which should be used to refine the cost budget. Advance quotations from equipment suppliers are often requested; these can be helpful provided they match the specification and are unbiased and explicit as to what is included.

Refinement of the procurement strategy and the programme enable cash flows to be updated; this in turn becomes the basis for review of annual funding, which can lead to phasing of implementation to fit a particular corporate programme of capital expenditure.

While the cost plan is being evolved during this phase, the need arises to introduce 'change control' to the estimating procedures. The costs of proposed changes in project scope, design and timing should be calculated and compared with the budget estimates. This information should enable management, with an understanding of the causes, to decide whether to accept, modify or reject the changes.

The most difficult types of change to handle are exchange rate fluctuations and inflation, because they are out of the control of the project management. The cost plan should define how these risks should be dealt with in later phases. Normally, the currency of the host country of the project should be used — if, however, large proportions of the funding and expenditure for the project are to be denominated in another currency, that country's currency should be used. Inflation indices should be those of the country where the expenditure takes place or of the country where items of plant are manufactured.

There are two common methods for dealing with the presentation of inflation and exchange rate effects in estimates. The first, prevalent in building and public works in the UK, is to place most emphasis on a base date estimated for project control purposes. Actual costs are then de-escalated for comparison with the base date costs, and predictions of cash or final costs are separately accounted. The second method, used by international corporations, places a strong emphasis on cash flow in large capital expenditure programmes. A corporate view is taken on future inflation and exchange rate fluctuations; this is reflected in all aspects of the business including project estimating and appraisal. So, instead of using fixed exchange rates and base dates, all estimated project expenditures are based on predicted exchange and inflation rates.

Thus, all estimates reflect the company's prediction of final costs, and escalation and exchange rate changes become another heading in change lists and reconciliations. Either method can be used if it is compatible with normal practice in the organisation in question and applied consistently.

At the end of conceptual engineering, a report on all aspects of the work is normally prepared for the Client's approval. One section of the report comprises the cost plan, including the latest cost estimate, which should always be compatible with the latest design, procurement strategy, time scheduling etc. The cost section should include:

- project description and history
- project programme
- an estimate summary including contingency allowances and owners' costs
- cash flow profile
- major project risks, sensitivities and the accuracy of the estimate
- project scope, exclusions and assumptions
- reconciliation with previous estimates
- estimating methods
- design basis.

Project planning

The project master programme should be produced in this phase. Planning studies should be conducted at a sufficiently detailed level to allow reliable modelling of the work. These studies are a part of the conceptual design, cost planning and procurement work, and have to be flexible and interactive to accommodate change as the concept is developed. Studies at the right level assist the project team to understand and evaluate in time/resource/cost terms the consequences of a particular course of action.

The other planning task in this phase is the time scheduling and resourcing of the conceptual engineering work itself, as described in section 5.2. In projects with strong elements of technical development the design work is frequently iterative; hence, the work plan changes continually and the programme should be reviewed regularly.

The main topic to be addressed here, however, is the longer term project master plan. It is at this point in the project that the initial work breakdown structure (WBS) should be established. A typical example of a conceptual WBS is shown in Fig. 5.4. The process of identifying and defining the work elements within the project is a powerful means of bringing out potential problems or organisational conflicts. It also helps to ensure that all work has been identified at the initial stage, and that responsibility for that work has been assigned.

As the project plan is developed further, each activity within it should be a package of work with discrete objectives and deliverables, closely aligned with the procurement and contract strategies. These activities can be resourced by the application of a man-hour estimate, either in a simple linear basis over the duration of the item or as a set of complex resources which reflect the changing nature of resource levels during the span of that activity.

Although planning and analysis can be carried out manually for simple projects, the advent of inexpensive computer-based project management packages has enabled project managers to analyse more complex programmes and resource requirements very quickly on a 'what if?' basis. Such conceptual resource planning is preliminary and can only provide an indication of the possible management problems that lie ahead. Details such as working patterns, shifts and holidays would not normally be addressed at this stage in the project, except perhaps those that have a major influence on progress — for example, weather patterns in marine projects.

In summary, an evaluation of conceptual planning should consider the following questions.

- Is there a WBS on which all planning, estimating and reporting are based?
- Does the engineering group have a defined set of objectives in terms of time and deliverables?
- Is the frequency of project progress review compatible with the timescale of the work?
- Is the planning and resource requirement of the next phase of the project being studied and modelled in sufficient detail?
- Have resource requirements been identified clearly to allow adequate time for their procurement or reallocation in the next phase of the project?

76

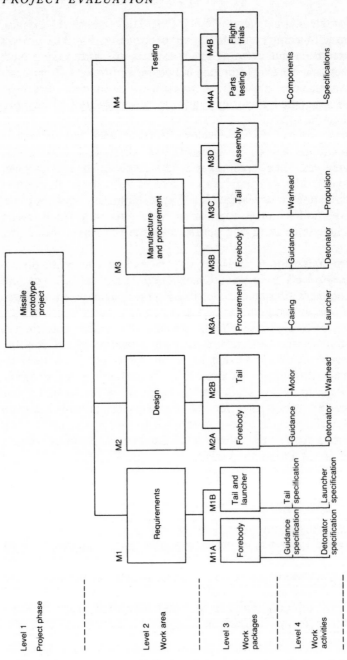

Level 1
Project phase

Level 2
Work area

Level 3
Work packages

Level 4
Work activities

Fig. 5.4. Conceptual work breakdown structure

Project procedures

Procedures for project administration, engineering and contract management should be included in the project plan. For small projects, brief procedures may be sufficient; for complex projects a comprehensive set of procedures should be prepared as part of the project quality assurance system. The following paragraphs relate to the latter context. Most of the procedures should be written before the end of conceptual engineering. They should be accompanied by the project execution plan which, updated as necessary, will describe the objectives, scope of work, responsibilities and organisation. The content of the procedures manual should be related to the type of contracts envisaged; for example, procedures intended to be followed by the project management team would be different from procedures imposed in a design-and-build contract, which are in effect contractual requirements.

These procedures are often extensive, and to be effective require considerable effort and thought in their compilation. If they have to be specially drafted in their entirety, sufficient time must be allocated in the project programme. Fortunately, they are usually based on existing standard documents used by the Client or by project management (if separate from the Client). Minor amendments to the standard documents may be needed to suit the specific project, but the changes could be expected to be confined to, say, 10% of the procedures. Some Clients may occasionally insist on using their standard procedures unamended. It is not unknown for these to be so complex as to limit the selection of designers and contractors to those with previous experience of operating the system — not always a satisfactory situation from the project standpoint.

The procedures must have the following qualities:

- they should be written
- they should be easy to assimilate and to implement for all participants
- they should enable the project to be controlled, but should not control the project
- they should not limit freedom of action unnecessarily
- they should bring order and efficiency to the administration of the project without placing such a burden of compliance

that participants are unduly diverted from their primary function.

These procedures should also include the following.

Co-ordination procedures. These should outline the frequency and formats of project meetings and reports. Emphasis should be on reporting by exception, with the use of graphics to record progress. Projects can be swamped by reporting of requirements; the objective should be to make essential information available without placing onerous requirements on participants. Reports should be succinct, easy to produce and easy to assimilate. Where detailed information is required, separate reports of limited distribution should be used.

Contract and procurement procedures. These should define standard formats for the preparation of contracts and purchase orders and procedures for tendering, evaluation and award. Procedures for contract administration may also be included. Procurement procedures should include requirements for inspection, certification, expediting and shipping, and for control of supplier data.

Cost control procedures. These will depend on the forms of contract being administered, but should cover budget formulation, cash flow, commitments/expenditures and sample formats. Costs may be reported against each contract or coded according to the Client's system. Such a system, based on the operation of the Client's business, may cut across technical and contractual interfaces and may be difficult for third parties to implement. Requirements for general accounting functions inclusive of commercial terms, formulae, invoicing procedures, funding, interest charges, currency and fluctuations, audits etc. may be included or may be the subject of a separate accounting procedure.

Document and drawing numbering systems. These should be prepared for large projects; they impose a common numbering and reference system on all drawings, specifications, reports, correspondence and other documents.

Change order procedures. These should define the way in which changes to the scope of work are to be managed. The procedure should specify the input required from those responsible for design, construction, cost and programme before approval and change order implementation. The cost coding of changes should also be defined.

Contract planning procedures. These should specify the planning system. The requirements for inputs from participants to the project master programme(s) should be given, together with the level of detail and resourcing expected in their own planning documents.

Engineering procedures. These should establish the standardisation of drawings, specifications and calculations, and approval procedures. The engineering manual should also list principal codes and standards and cover procedures for technical input to other departments such as procurement or construction.

Quality assurance manual. This should establish procedures to ensure planned and systematic actions so that the specified technical requirements are met. The QA manual will be integrated with other procedures, particularly engineering. Attention should be paid to review, checking and approval of the technical documentation and the management of technical interfaces between work packages and between technologies. The manual should also include provision for technical audits.

Construction and commissioning procedures. These should be prepared in outline at this stage. The detailed procedures, including quality control, should be available at the time of tendering. The application of construction procedures is discussed in chapters 7 and 8.

Material control procedures. These should specify the stock numbering system, which should be established and integrated with design at the commencement of the detailed engineering phase. Procedures for receipt storage and issue of materials should be given.

Approvals

The preparation of a report for the Client towards the end of this phase is mentioned above. In contrast to the earlier reporting and study stages, it should represent a clear statement of exactly how the project will be implemented in all its aspects. For an industrial project, the document is often called simply 'the project report', and describes in detail process selection, engineering of the plant and services, the proposed procurement arrangements, construction, commissioning and training, as well as time schedules and itemised costs. All this is for review and approval by the Client and possibly by other parties — it may have quite an extensive circulation. It will also mention any major changes to project scope and content that may have arisen during this phase: it is assumed here that these will have been discussed with and approved by the Client through the medium of early drafts of sections of the report as well as other documents. Where design-and-build contracts are to be tendered and let on a performance specification, the report would form the brief for the Contractors and would be part of the Tender documents.

For architectural and building projects, the equivalent stage is the detailed plan report (various other titles are also used), which includes many working drawings: site and floor plans, cross-sections and typical details carrying enough information to fix in final form all the dimensions and the appearance, materials and finishes for both the buildings and site development. The drawings are accompanied by schedules and outline specifications, design criteria and so on. The detailed plan is almost always presented for approval, as being the concept design freeze point which should enable the production run of detailed drawings for construction to commence without further changes. In fact, any significant design changes from here on become progressively more costly and disruptive.

5.4 Risk analysis

As the design, estimates and programme are being defined, based on increasingly reliable and refined data, the use of quantitative risk analysis techniques is extended. For major projects, where appropriate, preliminary simulations as well as probabilistic studies can be made of areas of uncertainty. These analyses can be of significant benefit during the design optimisation process, and can help the Client to form his view on possible changes to the project concept.

During this phase project management should develop a risk management plan, which should provide input to the contract strategy and to the choice of suitable types of contract. The plan should also assist in deciding how the detailed design and construction work should be packaged, together with responsibilities and the allocation of risks to each party involved in the project.

The risk management plan should evaluate the many elements which remain undefined at the end of conceptual engineering and which relate to all the subsequent work through to final commissioning. It should be possible to allocate contingency sums to the cost estimates and include them within an envelope of 'maximum likely cost' — it would be important to state clearly the purpose of each contingency and how and when it would be used. Of course, the amount of such contingencies over and above the best estimate varies from project to project. To give an indication of the scale of the provision, the amount might be 10% for a 'repeat' project having no special supply or construction problems, but as high as 45% for some petrochemical, tunnelling, or marine projects even at this stage of engineering definition.

5.5 Review topics

In the conceptual engineering phase the conceptual design is produced together with the project plan for implementation. This phase provides the last opportunity for the Client to alter radically the concept or scope of work without incurring substantial delays and extra costs. A review of this phase should consider such questions as the following.

- Is the design organisation effective, and does it match the technical requirements of the project?
- If the design organisation involves several firms, have they been adequately briefed? Is co-ordination between them effective?
- Is the project manager in post, with responsibility for the organisation and management of the whole of the work in this phase?
- Is there an effective procedure for the exchange of technical/ design information between designs firms or departments as required? Does the design optimisation take into account all the conflicting or interactive factors?
- Is the WBS (work packaging) for detailed design adequately defined and scheduled? Does it match the proposed procurement strategy?
- Has the procurement strategy been laid down, taking into account:
  - all technical requirements
  - sources of supply
  - items to be supplied separately from the construction contract
  - items to be imported

- o relationships between design and construction
- o types of contract
- o time scheduling?

- Has the project plan been updated? Does it define how the various aspects are to be reconciled and co-ordinated; e.g. design, procurement, construction, time schedule and cost plan?
- Does the cost plan show how the estimated costs are built up and related to WBS and to physical areas of the project as appropriate?
- Does the cost plan cover the following:

  - o projected amounts and timing of funding
  - o anticipated cash flow
  - o contingency allowances (and reasons for them)
  - o sensitivity analysis
  - o statement as to the accuracy of the estimates?

- Has the procedures manual been compiled? Does it cover all aspects of planning, control, reporting, communications and review?
- Have effective procedures been agreed and enforced for the following items (among others):
  - o order and control of changes in design or scope of work
  - o quality assurance?

6 Detailed design phase

6.1 Introduction

This chapter discusses the activities in the detailed design period, with the aim of identifying the questions that an evaluation of this phase should consider. Sections cover the approach to detailed design, design control, design and construction overlaps and relevant aspects of tendering procedures for construction contracts.

It is necessary to distinguish betwen evaluation of the design process and evaluation of the project as a whole in this phase. In the detailed design process, the design work in a particular engineering discipline, say air conditioning systems, can be appraised only by engineers experienced in that discipline. Of course, an engineer without such experience can pose a question such as 'Why did the air conditioning engineer not ensure that his duct work would not clash with structure and other services?'; but would find it very difficult to say with any real precision whether or not the air conditioning system as designed is adequate to its expected duty. The quality of the design therefore rests primarily with the professional engineers working in their own fields. Any competent design organisation must both deploy competent staff and provide for their work to be checked and reviewed at all stages. It is noted that legislation, particularly in Health and Safety, has increased the likelihood that where serious errors have been made the individuals responsible could be subject to legal action.

The evaluation of the design process, whether before or after the event, focuses not on the design itself but on the quality control procedures and measures taken to secure its success, including clear objectives; team composition; co-ordination between disciplines; adequate time, funds and staff for checking and review, etc.

Mistakes discovered at later stages can be very costly; the petrochemical industry, for example, goes to great lengths to impose quality assurance procedures.

The evaluation of the project as a whole at this stage would be concerned with the factors outlined above, but would also deal with broader issues, notably whether the intention of the project plan was being maintained through detailed design or whether aspects of it should be reconsidered. The project may be vulnerable with respect to the following questions.

- Are the design briefs to the design firms or departments concerned complete, including definition of the required output, and issued sufficiently early?
- Is there adequate provision for co-ordination and information exchange between these firms?
- At what point does the design become the responsibility of a construction contractor?

Conceptual engineering is often allowed to overlap the detailed design phase to an undefined degree; this in turn prevents a firm baseline being laid down for subsequent change control. These factors should be taken into account in the approach to the detailed design work.

6.2 The approach to detailed design

During this stage there should be no need to call the design concept into question, but if it is found to be deficient in some way two courses of action are possible:

- terminate detailed design; revert to an earlier project phase, such as feasibility or conceptual engineering, depending on the significance of the problem
- continue detailed design if the problem with the concept can be isolated and resolved without a major impact on design progress generally.

However, both courses of action would require a review of the project plan to identify and minimise the impact on final cost and completion date.

The detailed design process usually requires significant increase in the number of design personnel on the project to handle the increased volume of work. The value of the previously formulated contract strategy, management systems and procedures should become apparent. Any significant deviation from prescribed objectives in terms of progress, quality or cost should be detected quickly through the established reporting system by the project management, who should take appropriate action. Such review and action where necessary should be a regular activity conducted at weekly, biweekly or monthly intervals depending on the design period and the individual activity duration.

The contracts for detailed design

As noted in chapter 5, a single design organisation is frequently responsible for both the conceptual and the detailed phases. For larger projects, at home or overseas, the detailed design may be too large a task for a single firm, or may require specialised knowledge. In such situations, separate contracts for detailed design may be needed; the types of contract should have been decided in the previous phase. Where necessary, competent design firms should also have been shortlisted, so that the awards of contract and mobilisation of the teams can proceed quickly.

It is important that both the firms and their contracts are matched to the task, as scope for change is limited once the work is under way. Only in exceptional circumstances, for instance where the designer is seriously underperforming, should substitution of another organisation be considered. The project disruption in terms of time and cost could be considerable as the replacement organisation would have to start its work with no prior project knowledge. The alternative, less disruptive route is to supplement the designer's areas of weakness and/or underperformance. This may be imposed as an action on the designer's management, for example to subcontract part of the work, associated with increased project management surveillance. Alternatively, project management may wish to inject its own resources into the designer's team using personnel known and trusted to ensure delivery of acceptable results. This approach, however, must be handled carefully to avoid diluting and confusing the contractual responsibility of the design organisation.

In some circumstances it may be much easier to change the designer's form of contract, as the following example illustrates. There being a well-defined scope of work to modify and extend an existing facility, a designer accepted the detailed design on a lump sum basis. It transpired, however, that the Client-supplied drawings of the existing facility showed significant discrepancies from the actual position in matters of detail. The Client could not or would not recognise such discrepancies, the resolution of which required the designer to expend extra time and cost, as a difficulty. This expenditure eroded partly or completely any margin built in to the lump sum price. The designer therefore minimised his own costs and looked for other ways of securing recompense by rigidly interpreting and applying his contract. This detracted from the main design impetus and delayed construction, resulting in a disproportionate increase in construction costs.

The transfer of risk from designer to Client, by rendering the contract form closer to a reimbursable basis for some elements of the work, would have retained and encouraged the designer's co-operation and positive commitment to maintaining the project programme. In the event, such a change was not accepted by the Client; much project management time was spent cajoling a reluctant designer to perform in the interests of the project.

This real-life example is an extreme case, but one that illustrates that having and maintaining an appropriate design contract basis is necessary to project success.

Management systems for project control

The detailed design phase represents the period of greatest design activity and also requires, therefore, much increased effort in the control of cost and time. If the design contracts are fixed price, the cost control systems should place emphasis on containing the costs against the contracts. The planning systems should be milestone based and aimed at ensuring timely distribution of design drawings to the construction Contractor and submission of specifications and requisitions to the equipment and material vendors. If the design contracts contain cost-reimbursable elements, the costs should be controlled against the predetermined budgets in the design cost plans.

Detailed design cannot be evaluated without control data. In order to provide the required information, the project control system should include the following elements for a large or complex project:

- planning system at key levels of management control with

drawings and documents schedules at the lowest level
- cost control system that links design labour resources or costs to the planning system as well as related procurement cost on an area basis through the WBS
- change control system that formalises the recording and control of changes to the designer's scope of work
- man-hour control system that allocates labour cost to the WBS
- funding control system linked to the cost and planning system so as to anticipate future project fund requirements
- capital cost control system to ensure that the facilities are being designed within the overall project cost plan.

The system may be computer based or manual as required, but should provide both Client and Contractor with the information needed to manage the project actively. The key to successful detail design management systems is the establishment of the WBS that allocates responsibility for each element of design work or cost to an individual. This structure would be a more detailed breakdown than the outline shown in Fig. 5.4. The lack of such clear budget assignment is often the cause of serious project overruns in detail design.

The cost control system for detailed design activities on a large project is inevitably oriented to the control of labour costs. However, in the case of contracts that require the Contractor to procure materials and equipment it is necessary to have an integrated WBS that also defines the coding structure for all cost and progress reporting.

It is not appropriate in this volume to describe project management control systems in detail. Many systems are available; in order to be effective the selected system should have certain qualities. These were discussed at some length in section 5.3. However, the systems now have to handle a much larger volume of information; hence the following requirements.

- The frequency of reporting should suit the pace of the project.
- Management reports should be structured hierarchically and should be available at varying levels of detail to those individuals responsible for the work.
- Reports should be forward-looking, clear and consistent in format, and as selective as possible so as to be easily assimilated.
- Reports should not hide or disguise adverse trends in progress

and cost. The review process should always allow for a double pass of information. The first pass would illustrate the results of the project update without the influence of rescheduling; the second pass would show the new plan of action needed to achieve the project objectives.

Management and engineering procedures

The formal procedures initiated in the concept design stage remain relevant as the work proceeds. They should be reviewed early in the project when personnel have had time to experience their operation, and at regular intervals thereafter to take account of changing requirements as the project organisation evolves from phase to phase.

After detailed design has started, lines of communications tend to become stretched as the numbers of personnel and external organisations engaged increase. The procedures should ensure smooth and efficient transfer of management or technical information, internally between designers or externally with other parties. Failure of this transfer could result in abortive work that frustrates the participants once it is discovered and jeopardises the programme. Accordingly, the transfer of information from the originator for 'action', 'approval', 'comment' or 'information only' should be organised in a formal manner and monitored by regular meetings. The considerable volume of paper generated during a detailed design even on small projects should be transmitted in the appropriate detail and quantity according to a project distribution matrix typified by Fig. 6.1.

6.3 Design implementation

A review of detailed design in a real situation will consider the following aspects of a project, which are not generally encountered before this phase.

Personnel and organisation

The bulk of detailed design work is a production effort, and is preferably conducted on a task force basis. The design group should be organised in a dedicated team, located ideally in a project-specific office where distractions from the designer's other business activities are minimised. By this means the detailed design team creates its own identity, which tends to motivate everybody

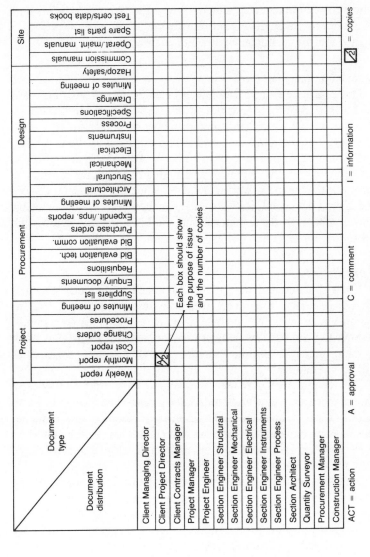

Fig. 6.1. Standard distribution list for project documents

concerned, whether in one office or several. Team members should be organised with each understanding his or her role through defined lines of communication to the designer's Project Manager. The Project Manager should be the single point of contact with the Client, through whom all formal communications of a managerial or technical nature are focused.

Detailed design brief

The completeness of the design briefs in the project plan was raised in section 6.1. Certainly these should provide the design teams with such project information as background history to date, strategy, and time and cost budgets. Definition of the tasks may need to be expanded in detail; it may be best if the design teams themselves then assemble all pertinent information necessary to carry out the technical work. The detailed design brief so produced and agreed between Client and designer then becomes the principal source of design data, criteria and methods for all existing and subsequently engaged project personnel.

Design freeze

When the detailed design has advanced sufficiently that the 'design integrity' is assured, it is advisable to impose a detailed design freeze on the whole project or part of it. This step should be formally imposed by project management to ensure that work on the project will continue smoothly and that project programmes will be maintained.

The design freeze makes everyone aware that the general arrangement drawings and specification cannot be changed. It also helps to shut out questions of engineering preference, thus reducing unnecessary expenditure of time and cost. The design should be fit for the purpose intended if it has been developed in accordance with the concept.

Occasions will arise, however, when the design freeze must be relaxed. There should be a formal change order procedure to deal with this, specifying the criteria for and management of the change. Typically, a request for a design change at this stage should only be considered for specific reasons, for example

- to maintain design integrity and/or operability
- for safety reasons

- to meet supplier equipment or material features
- to satisfy statutory authority requirements
- to achieve an overall saving in project cost or time.

Once the need for a change is accepted, it should be implemented properly, taking the effects on time, cost, resources and other design areas into account. The flow chart shown in Fig. 6.2 summarises

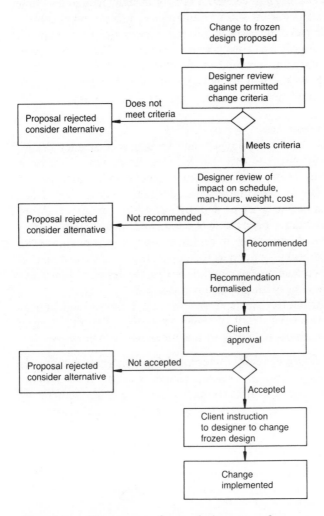

Fig. 6.2. Change to a frozen design: procedure

the decision points and courses of action necessary to manage design change properly.

6.4 Contract strategy

It was noted in chapter 5 that the procurement strategy should be decided and incorporated into the project plan, this work being part of conceptual engineering. As major design changes and time slippages can occur in the present phase, project management should be prepared to review and if necessary to modify the contract strategy for supply and construction. Sections 5.2 and 5.3 showed how some contracting procedures and types of contract permit more flexibility than others. The decisions made earlier about types of contracts should have taken such factors into account.

Design and construction overlap

The deliberate overlapping of the later stages of detailed design with the early stages of construction is a device which has been used for many years, to shorten the project development period and bring a high value product into production earlier, or having been preplanned as part of a design-and-build contract. More recently, a virtue has been made of design and construction overlap in the 'fast track' approach to building. For present purposes the fast track method is defined as the appointment of a construction contractor to commence work while a separate design organisation is still proceeding with the detailed design.

Whether or not the overlap is preplanned, it imposes additional requirements on the detailed design process. A design reviewer will be most interested in such questions as the following.

- Does the designer fully understand the construction methods that could be used for various elements of the design? (This has particular relevance to the overlap case where temporary integrity of a partly constructed design must be assured.)
- Does the design incorporate preferred methods and details offered by the Contractor, thus entailing potential time and cost benefits?
- Does the designer fully appreciate the need to adopt a possibly unfamiliar sequence of design development to meet the demands of the construction programme, and the extra effort that may be involved?

- Does the fast track route result in a shorter project timescale?
- If the timescale is shortened, what design decisions have been based on engineering judgements where precise details are not available? How effective is design co-ordination in this area?
- Has the process of designing for ease and speed of construction resulted in loss of economy?

Finally, the fast track method requires a spirit of co-operation and problem-solving. If its use was not preplanned it may not fit into an existing structure of contracts.

6.5 Tendering procedures

In general, there are four stages in tendering for construction contracts: selection of tenderers; invitations to bid; tender preparation and delivery; and appraisal of tenders, negotiation and decision. The award of contract then follows. In a situation where the detailed design is executed by design specialists separately from the construction contract(s), the designers usually have a strong technical input to the appraisal of tenders for construction.

Where contractors are to be selected to undertake both detailed design and construction, on the basis of the conceptual engineering, the conceptual designers ought to be involved in the tender appraisal process. The tenderers' proposed arrangements for the detailed design work are a critical element in their ability to fulfil the project objectives.

We are concerned here with evaluation of the tendering process, and particularly with questions influencing the way the design is implemented in construction. Some of the questions below might be raised early in the tendering process; others as part of an evaluation at a later date. They are additional to those given in section 5.3 under *'Procurement strategy'*.

Concerning the pre-tender period

- How is the tendering process to be managed on behalf of, or by, the Client? Who is responsible?
- Do the procedures and documents ensure that only competent contractors will be selected?
- Are the proposed types of contracts in accordance with the project plan? If not, have the changes been thought through?
- Do the designs and specifications issued for tender purposes

describe the work adequately for the proposed types of contracts?
- Do they match the other tender documents? Do they provide a basis for free and fair competition?
- Do the designs and specifications show that the designer has fulfilled his obligations under his design contract?
- If the detailed designs are not complete:

  o are the omissions clearly stated?
  o are the provisions to complete them explicit?

- Do the tender documents specify any design work which is to be carried out under the contract?
- Are quality assurance requirements stated?
- Are the provisions for approval of contractors' designs, equipment and materials laid down?
- Are the contractors' responsibilities clear as regards implementing the design in practice?
- Are the contractors' responsibilities for subsuppliers similarly clear?
- Do the instructions to tenderers specify the documents and data to be submitted?

Concerning the tender appraisal period

- Has a satisfactory procedure for appraisal been written and agreed?
- Have all tenderers received the same additional information if any has been issued during the tender period?
- Have the following aspects of the tenders been appraised: technical compliance; project organisation, staff and procedures; the execution plan, programme and resources; materials sources; subcontracting arrangements; project control methods; quality assurance and control; plant schedule; current workload etc?
- Has the commercial appraisal of tenders covered such necessary elements as:

  o sufficiency of tender
  o arithmetical checks
  o bill of quantities/whether each item is priced/dayworks schedule

- o cash flow
- o insurances
- o compliance with contract conditions
- o extent of qualifications of tender
- o potential for claims?

- If there is more than one contract:

  - o how are the interfaces covered
  - o what are the arrangements for co-ordinating the contracts
  - o which party carries the responsibility?

- How are the contracts to be managed?
- What risks are associated with each tender including potential claims? How are these to be offset?
- How do the tenders compare with respect to maintainability of the completed works and implications for 'whole life costs'?

As regards cost, the project estimates should have been updated just before tender stage; the tenders are compared with them. If the tenders are over budget some rethinking is obviously required to effect a reconciliation before the contract is awarded.

6.6 Post-design services

This type of service belongs strictly to the contruction phase, but is mentioned here because the services of the design organisation may continue post-contract, after the design has reached 'approved for construction' status. Indeed, in some industries, notably civil engineering and building, it is traditional for the design organisation to continue its involvement in a construction supervisory capacity. However, it is common in the petrochemical industry to engage a different organisation for contruction supervision and management from that pursuing the detailed design: in this case the design organisation may have to provide a post-contract involvement sometimes known as 'general supervision'.

Whichever route is taken, designer representation will be required during the construction phase, to maintain the design intent and hence the integrity of the project by dealing with equipment or materials approvals involving design issues and other matters of interpretation.

During construction, the design organisation is normally represented by a small team covering the essential technical specialisations. The team should not be concerned with routine approvals of fabrication drawings, equipment or materials, which should be handled under the normal arrangements for contract supervision. It should deal, rather, with queries requiring design advice or interpretation, routed to it by the project manager or his staff. The queries are registered and evaluated by the appropriate technical specialists. Action is decided according to the type of query, which may be:

- requiring advice — no impact on design
- requiring resolution — possibly has impact on design
- requiring resolution — impact on construction possibly giving rise to a contract variation order.

Appropriate action is agreed and the response is returned to the query originator.

6.7 Review topics

The quality of the design process depends both on the technical expertise of the designers and on the organisation of the work. Evaluation of the accuracy and quality of design in a particular technical branch of engineering is a matter for engineers experienced in that branch. A review of the detailed design phase should consider questions such as the following (arising from the analysis and advice given in this chapter).

- Are the design briefs complete? Were they issued sufficiently early to the firms or departments concerned?
- Are the design firms well-matched to the tasks? Are their contract conditions suitable? Do they enable the work to be executed smoothly?
- Is there an effective procedure for information exchange and co-ordination between the organisations or departments involved?
- Does the WBS define responsibilities and boundaries between the tasks?
- Are the control systems related to the WBS? What measures do they cover (e.g. control of time, cost, man-hours, design changes)?
- Is there an effective procedure for updating, reporting and controlling project capital costs during design development?

- Are the arrangements for design quality control satisfactory? Who is responsible? Are sufficient competent staff and programme time provided for this checking activity?
- Are the quality assurance procedures working adequately?
- Has the design intent of the conceptual phase been maintained without alteration?
- What design changes (within the general concept) have occurred during detailed design? How were they recorded and controlled? What were the reasons for them?
- Has the detailed design programme been maintained?
- Has the contracts policy for construction been confirmed?
- Is the design completed (or to be completed) before the commencement of construction — if not, the following questions arise:

  o what is the extent of the overlap (between design and contruction)
  o how is the issue of construction drawings planned and monitored
  o are the designers aware of the implications for their work
  o does the overlap method accord with the contracts structure and conditions
  o if unplanned at concept stage, has the cost effect of overlap on design and construction been evaluated and accepted?

- Are the tendering and tender appraisal procedures satisfactory (see the list of questions in section 6.5)?

7 Procurement and construction

As procurement and construction are closely connected in practice, this chapter deals with both, devoting one section to each.

7.1 Procurement

Introduction

The first part of the procurement cycle, described in chapter 5, covers the responsibility for procurement together with the strategy, financing and organisation. The cycle then moves to the identification and placing of orders for long lead items. By the beginning of the detailed design phase, the responsibility for supply of each item has been defined and other documents are being prepared — supplier lists, prequalification procedures and enquiries. Then, as the design and materials schedules are finalised, orders are placed for main equipment items and bulk purchase requisitions are raised. Thus, the procurement cycle may extend from the conceptual engineering phase through detailed design to fabrication and construction.

This section does not discuss construction contracts, although they are a part of procurement; it is concerned with the identification and purchasing of items of manufacturing, process or other plant or equipment and materials (for a large factory project, for example), whose supply in general does not form part of the construction contracts. These supply orders can represent as much as 40% of the project budget. The planning, expediting and monitoring of the numerous orders to meet the project programme is often intractable, as purchasing staff well know, whether in clients' or contractors' offices. A review of procurement should ascertain whether the purchasing activities have been properly organised and documented.

Purchasing starts with the agreement of supplier lists, mentioned above, and continues until the suppliers receive final payment. The flowcharts in Figs 7.1 and 7.2 show these activities and the deliverables for which each participant is responsible. The cycle does not vary greatly with size, the principles of handling 100 or 10 000 orders being the same. In the latter case, however, the complexities arising from sheer numbers or from the involvement of a number of countries would require a different organisation to do the work.

It should be noted that the purchasing function follows a similar cycle when it is the responsibility of a main contractor as part of his construction contract.

Approved supplier lists

The procurement plan establishes the broad scope of supply and breakdown of the whole materials and equipment requirement into packages. Within this framework, lists of approved suppliers for all items are prepared, considering all other relevant factors, such as the project location and the specification. Some companies may be required to prequalify for inclusion on the lists. Such prequalification should include technical and commercial evaluations of the supplier's corporate structure and organisation, financial status, resources and present workload, systems for quality assurance and control, and relevant experience, both generally and in previous work for the Client. The supplier's ability to meet the political, legal and security requirements of the 'project country' should also be checked.

Once the supplier lists have been approved by the Client for each category of materials and equipment, they should not be amended except with the Client's approval and under strict guidelines.

Tender and award

A review of this part of the cycle should consider first whether the following basic objectives are being met by the purchasing system:

- that all supply items are related to the overall plan
- that the system defines the time schedule, cost budget and purchase conditions for each item

99

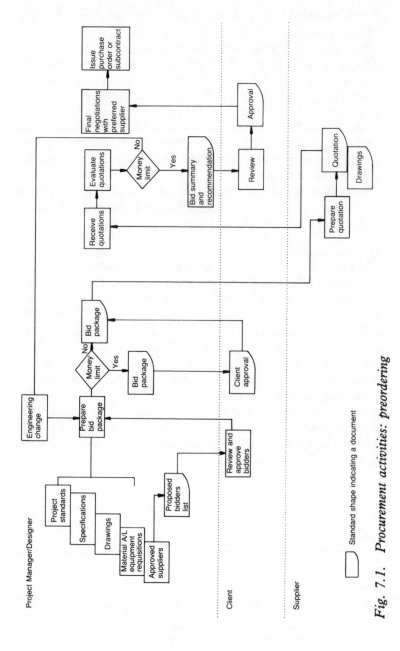

Fig. 7.1. Procurement activities: preordering

100

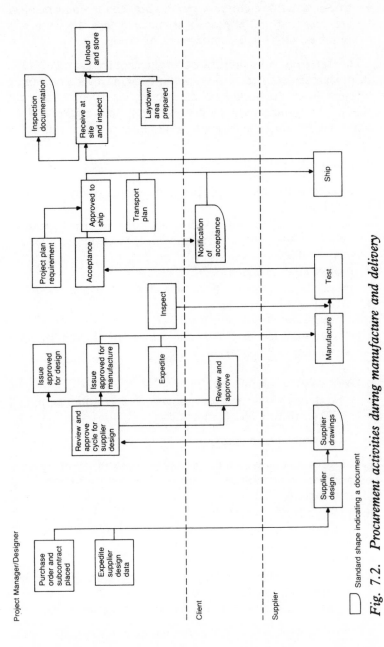

Standard shape indicating a document

Fig. 7.2. Procurement activities during manufacture and delivery

- that in each case all necessary evaluations and recommendations are prepared and approvals obtained before the issue of a purchase order and commitment of funds.

The first step is the preparation of the enquiry package. Here, the procurement team is responsible for bringing together the input required from the designers, the project management and the Client. The enquiry package should contain information and the requirements which the supplier has to meet in his quotation, as follows.

Information. The required information comprises:

- all necessary technical data, drawings, specifications and project standards
- the scope of the work with description of the equipment (including spare parts) and a materials schedule for the purchase of bulk items
- project equipment numbering system
- project procedures for document numbering and control
- conditions of purchase
- standard purchase order form
- a programme for the provision of design data required by other parties and for deliveries to site
- proformas for tendering
- base date for pricing
- general information on site conditions, location, utilities supply, local contractors and laydown areas.

Requirements. These comprise:

- supplier documentation, including scheduling of specific performance details, maintenance requirements and consumables
- quality assurance systems
- quality control, inspection and testing arrangements
- bonds and guarantees
- insurances
- instructions for packaging, protection, marking, shipping and any space or size limitations
- training provisions and attendance for commissioning.

Following approval of the enquiry package, it should be issued to an agreed number of suppliers selected from the approved list. The governments of some countries are very wary of this 'shortlisting' method; the existence of an 'approved suppliers' list for a given category of work sometimes leads to the decision that all the listed suppliers be given the opportunity to supply except for any who are proved to be overloaded or completely unable to comply with specialised requirements. Be that as it may, the aim is to invite and receive genuine tenders, i.e. quotations from reputable suppliers who are competent in all senses of the word.

With this in view, they should always be given a reasonable time to prepare and submit their bids, including time for seeking any clarifications. Strict rules and procedures should cover both technical and commercial aspects of the opening and evaluation of tenders and the award of orders.

The appraisal of each supplier's bid should obviously be conducted objectively by competent personnel, and should cover the aspects described in section 6.5. These can be summarised as follows:

- conformity with all the requirements of the enquiry
- supplier's qualifications — i.e. limitations or caveats, technical or commercial, made by the supplier in his tender
- restraints in programme terms
- technical acceptability.

In most situations it is convenient to make the commercial and financial analysis first, resulting in a list of commercially acceptable tenders; these are then subjected to technical scrutiny.

The results of the evaluation should be documented in an agreed form, recommending one or more preferred suppliers for consideration. Points which require negotiation before the order can be finalised should also be enumerated.

The purchase order system used may be based on established procedures within the Client's organisation, or more appropriately may be as used by the design or project management organisation. The in-house purchasing documentation and procedures of most client organisations are geared to consumables, spares and bought-in components, and are not suitable for purchases of the magnitude and complexity involved in major projects.

As a minimum, the purchase order should contain all the information and requirements listed above in the enquiry package.

These should be brought up do date so as to include all negotiated variations to the enquiry package, covering the final commerical and technical conditions.

Expediting

The organisation and system expediting (following up an order after it has been placed) should be designed:

- to anticipate problems before delays occur
- to exert pressure where necessary to ensure that programmes are kept
- to provide forewarning of changes to programme dates so that appropriate action can be taken.

Expediting of materials and equipment supplies is normally done selectively. Judgement is required in selecting which orders should be expedited and in choosing the frequency, methods and resources utilised; the latter may include external agencies. Expediting should cover not only the manufacture and delivery of the equipment, but also the submission by the supplier of technical data and placing of suborders, which are often just as critical in achieving project completion. Staff involved in expediting must use care and discretion. Their brief should be to obtain technical and progress information to which the purchaser is entitled. They must not give any instructions on their own account, for obvious contractual reasons. However, the customer who expedites regularly and hard is more likely to have promised deliveries fulfilled.

Quality control and inspection

The foundation of these operations is the project quality plan, which relates to quality assurance. Implementation in both procurement and construction activities should be regulated by a detailed quality control plan and procedures.

The function of quality control and inspection is usually exercised by a section within the project team, which may be supported by specialist organisations contracted to provide inspection services. Often, especially on overseas projects, an independent inspectorate is engaged in addition to the project's internal quality control staff. The plan mentioned above should be the means of controlling and co-ordinating the work of all the organisations that are involved.

A reviewer of the arrangements for quality control and inspection would require answers to some fairly fundamental questions, such as the following.

- Is there a satisfactory quality control plan? Are all concerned familiar with it and following it?
- How do responsibilities for quality control flow from the Client through to the suppliers?
- Are the levels of quality control required clear? Are the systems of reporting and documentation providing the required information?
- What authority is delegated to participating organisations (especially concerning suspension of work and corrective action)?
- Has the correct amount of responsibility been delegated to individual managers, engineers and inspectors at all levels? Do they understand their roles?
- Are the lines of communication and reporting from inspectors to the central quality control office independent and capable of giving accurate, rapid feedback?

Transport of materials and equipment items

The project requirements for packing, marking, shipping, insurance and delivery are included in the purchase order documentation. Specific problems, such as heavy lifts and items of exceptional size should have been considered during design; arrangements for these should now be finalised. The procedures for the receipt of goods and formal transfer of responsibility for care and insurances at the construction site should be co-ordinated with the organisation responsible for materials control, and the laydown areas should be designated.

Supplier documentation

The timing and formats for documentation to be provided by the suppliers should always be specified in the enquiry and confirmed in the purchase order. However, this obligation is often underestimated by the suppliers in terms of technical input, volume and cost.

First, there is the provision of technical data for design of services and other interfacing elements. As mentioned in section 5.3, this

105

is often required at an early stage: delays or lack of information here can not only prejudice the progress of the supply items to which the information relates, but can also affect the entire project programme. Second, the suppliers are required to submit data for approval, followed later by material certification, inspection reports and so on. Finally, commissioning schedules, operating and maintenance manuals and spare parts lists are essential to the Client's future operations — their preparation, to the Client's standards, can represent a considerable effort which comes late in the programme and is a frequent source of friction.

Invoicing and payment
The methods and procedures for the invoicing by and payments to suppliers, specified in the purchase order, should ensure, among other aspects, that:

- the approval route is as short as practicable
- the suppliers understand the documentation and routing of invoices that is to be followed.

The system should provide project management with accurate, fast, reporting of invoice status, funding and cash flow for comparison with the project cost plan.

7.2 Construction
In this section the evaluation of the construction phase is discussed, taking as an example an unspecified medium-to-large project, in which several contractors may be engaged under separate contracts. Other situations would present different pictures: a management contract, or indeed the common arrangement with a single contractor responsible for all construction and most of the procurement, are just two such examples. However, the differences between these situations relate only to how the work is to be done; they are mainly in contract terms and in the assignment of responsibility for managing the integration of many items from many sources into a coherent whole. In one case the Client's project management team might be responsible for procurement and co-ordination; at the other extreme these functions might be the total responsibility of the Contractor, with the Client's team taking a monitoring role. In both cases the functions to be performed are similar.

106

Most of the project budget is expended during the construction phase, certainly if equipment purchase is included. From the Client's point of view, 90% of the budget is committed once the contracts are placed; the cost control function now emphasises cost containment and reporting. Planning at all levels, of the contracts and contracted work, must also be effective.

The contracts should preferably have a clean start, with necessary design information and other documentation issued at the commencement where the contract so requires. The contrasting situation in which construction is overlapped with design is described in chapter 6. This drive for shorter timescales and shorter payback periods has many pitfalls, not least the division or overlapping of responsibilities involving Client, designers and contractors. The successful completion of the project on this basis is usually the product of joint planning, continual review, flexible contracts and, above all, first-class co-operation.

Whatever the situation, a reviewer must know the way in which the construction was planned, and how it is being organised, controlled and documented.

Planning for construction

As the emphasis in the work of the project changes from design towards construction, so this change affects the project management organisation. The task of managing the design is progressively reduced, and the construction management team has to be established. It is not unusual about this time for the Project Manager and some key staff to move to the site, because this is now the centre of the work.

Essential steps in planning for construction should be included in the project plan already prepared; these include the development of the procurement strategy, definition of construction work packages, draft contract documents, time schedules and cost plans. All this work has the aim of ensuring that contracts are placed at the times required by the master programme, and that the construction is properly managed from then on.

Figure 7.3 shows these steps, together with other activities which are related to the site and are now required before mobilisation takes place, and include the following tasks:

- prepare and agree the construction management organisation and appoint staff in key positions

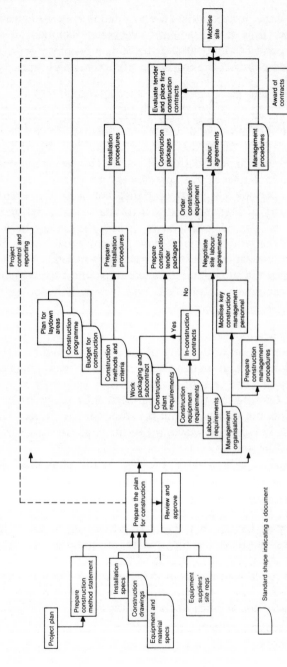

Fig. 7.3. Typical project activities: site mobilisation

- prepare construction management procedures covering such aspects as planning and reporting, change control, documentation, and cost and invoice control
- define policies and requirements for

  o labour agreements and industrial relations
  o provision of construction plant
  o provision of site facilities, including labour accommodation, laydown areas, communications systems
  o site safety and health

- prepare construction programme
- finalise construction cost budgets, itemised by cost-centre and by contracts; show contingency and escalation allowances.

Some of the above activities arise from the need to adopt certain common standards among the several independent contractors working on the same site. These standards must be set by the Client's project team in order to achieve efficient and harmonious operation without unnecessarily limiting the contractors' freedom of action.

Defining these standards will enable each contractor, when appointed, to be aware of the exact scope of his responsibilities for the work to be executed, which areas of the site are to be under his control, how co-ordination with other contractors is to be effected and what common facilities are provided.

Turning for a moment to the situation in which a single contractor is appointed for the whole construction, the reader may analyse which of the activities would in this case be undertaken by the Contractor — in fact, this amounts to bringing the 'award of contract' towards the left of Fig 7.3.

Arrangements for deployment and training of staff for the operation of the completed project works facility should also be settled, and the extent of the contractors' involvement defined. Finally, any restrictions affecting the contractors' possession of the site, or portions thereof, must be stated. Obviously, such matters are normally covered by the Contract conditions and are particularly significant if existing facilities are in operation at the site. Restrictions may also arise from the interest of, or agreements with, adjoining owners.

Change order procedure

The early stages of construction provide a fruitful source of delays, variations and potential contract claim situations that can arise in many ways. Of great interest in a review of the construction phase are the procedures for dealing with approvals and potential variations, and the manner in which they are managed.

Some examples of the ways in which the best laid plans can go wrong are listed below; these are chosen mainly because they may affect both design and construction, and may have contractual consequences:

- late request from the Client for a design change
- late request from the design office for a design change (this could happen especially, but not only, where overlap exists between design and construction)
- omissions, mistakes or inconsistencies in the construction contract drawings or documents
- unforeseen site conditions
- equipment offered by the Contractor that does not entirely meet the specification
- equipment offered that does not fit in the space provided
- changed method of construction
- design change for safety reasons.

(The above list may be compared with the reasons for changes at detailed design stage given in section 6.3).

Project management should decide how the response to these issues should be organised, what action should be taken, and how it should be documented. Questions which a reviewer in any particular case should consider comprise the following.

- Do adequate procedures exist for approvals, change control and reporting? Are they being implemented?
- Do the contractual relationships assist or inhibit the above process?
- Has responsibility been allocated for control, action and follow-up?
- How are potential changes in design or construction identified and resolved?
- How are the effects on time and cost taken into account?

Organisation for construction

In general, the Client, the Project Manager and the main Contractors each have their own organisation at the site. Where the Client has delegated the authority for management of the project, his representation may consist of a liaison officer only. For a major project, however, he may decide to do much of the contracts administration at the site, and would have quite an extensive organisation for that purpose. If the project is an extension of an existing facility, the operator or a user organisation would also be involved.

Figure 7.4 shows a typical situation in which the Client has appointed an independent firm to undertake the management of the project. All the principal functions which have been discussed are shown. In this case, a heavy load of planning, co-ordination and construction management is placed on the project team, because the supply and construction works are packaged as a number of separate contracts (compare Fig. 5.2(d)).

A review of a project in progress should consider the following questions about the construction organisation.

- Are all the necessary functions represented at the site? Who is responsible for each?
- Has authority been adequately delegated to those managing the work at various levels?
- Are personnel with the required expertise deployed? Have they been briefed as to their role and their interface with others?
- Are the construction management teams adequately staffed?
- How do the various site organisations relate to one another?
- Do individual managers understand their role and any contractual implications of their work?
- Are the procedures clearly written and being followed?

Another aspect of organisation is labour and labour relations. Particularly in a multi-contractor site, facilities such as messing, recreation and welfare are important; as are the control of the workforce, whole-site agreements and procedures affecting industrial relations, recruitment, trade unions and so on. It should never be forgotten that a single industrial dispute can wipe out the calculated profitability of an investment. Experience has shown that, in reviewing the organisation of construction and related

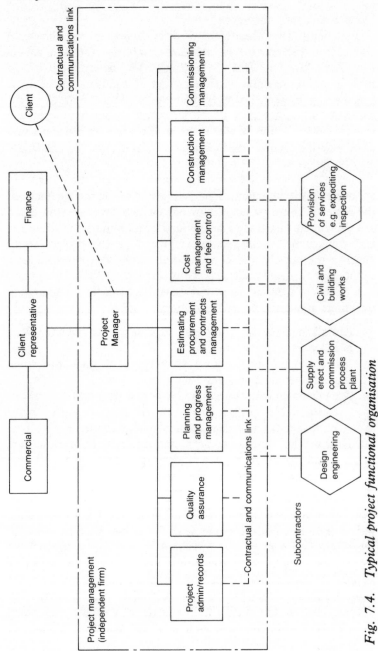

Fig. 7.4. Typical project functional organisation

activities, it should never be assumed that the basic necessities such as motivation, planning and co-ordination capability and procedures exist within the organisations involved.

Control of construction

If the parties involved — project management, site supervision and contractors' construction teams — are working well, control is exercised through knowing where to put the main effort at a given time and maintaining good communications. There are three aspects to be considered. These comments would apply equally to the Client's and the contractors' supervision.

Control of quality of materials and workmanship. Review the quality control plan and establish how well it is working through:

- individuals and their several responsibilities
- corporate responsibilities
- preset levels of quality control and inspection
- timing and content of documentation.

Control of cost and time. In most contracts, the price and time required to complete the specified scope of works are defined, and resources to be used are then scheduled in the construction plan. Control is thus a matter of reporting and regular progressing against fixed targets. If a slippage of time occurs, the base programme or target may have to be adjusted: a decision must be made as to whether it is less misleading in such a case to report against the original schedule or against a revised one. The base schedule should be revised only when this is necessary to avoid confusion in reporting or to accommodate the effects of significant change orders.

Construction planning must have the commitment of all concerned, reflect the agreed methods of construction, and be responsive to change. The method of progress measurement must be valid and credible to those who must manage the work. The progress reporting should be concise, concentrate on the critical areas, and be related to the agreed plan. Well-prepared reports are essential for busy people who do not have time to read voluminous documents; current good practice is based on management by exception, which avoids wasting people's time. A good reporting system is not a solution to the whole problem of control, as the attitudes of the contracting parties towards the control of cost and time are fundamentally different, being based on different objectives.

The control of cost in a lump sum contract would appear to be a simple matter, at least for the Client. The final cost is known in advance, unless war, insurrection or some other uncontrollable event occurs. The Client only needs to know at regular intervals that the Contractor is making due progress towards the completion of construction within the stated time.

The required information is usually in the form of monthly reports, related to a system of monthly interim payments. In the first few weeks of the contract, when the reporting system is being set up, there is sometimes a tug-of-war between the site supervision team and the Contractor. The former usually attempt to persuade the Contractor to supply detailed construction plans, work breakdowns, costings and programmes, so that he can be called to account for any delay or deviation later on. The Contractor is usually perfectly willing to provide whatever information is required by his contract, and probably more than is required. On the other hand, he must maintain flexibility to modify his plans in detail. Under a lump sum contract, he is carrying all the risks of the construction phase and is not normally bound to reveal in detail how he has planned time and cost contingencies in relation to those risks.

It is concluded that the disparity, if not actual conflict, of commercial objectives is bound to be reflected in the information passed between the contracting parties. The experienced Contractor will offer a programme of work as his contractual commitment, and report progress on that basis. This programme may well be different from his own working programme, although the final result is the same — i.e. to complete the work or sections of the work by the contract dates.

In more difficult situations, not necessarily only in lump sum contracts, the Contractor's working programme may be geared to a completion date later than than nominated in the contract. As a hypothetical illustration, the Contractor may have perceived a high probability that delays will occur beyond his control, which in contractual terms would justify an extension of time without penalty. An example is marine or offshore works, where all programming is subject to weather conditions. If the Contractor has confidence in his assessment of the risks, he would be commercially prudent to plan his commitment of resources on the assumption that some delay will occur. At the same time, he cannot assume relief from a contractual responsibility by basing his reports on such a hypothesis in advance of the event. Thus, circumstances may arise where what is reported during construction does not exactly match what is going on. Plans, particularly contingency plans, may be concealed or disguised, for commercial reasons connected with the way the contract is operated. The concealment may be on either side; the Client's or the Contractor's.

In considering the questions to be addressed in a review of the construction phase, one topic which may arise is related to methods of estimating costs. In many types of contract, the Contractor's tender rates and prices are used to determine the cost to the Client of changes or variations in the quantities of work done. The method of measurement and of application of the rates depends upon the type of contract, but the use of the tender rates enables the effect of the changes to be related easily to the original cost plan. The resulting change in the total price to be paid by the Client can be accurately predicted, and in most cases argument as to the rates themselves is avoided.

The use of tender rates to assess the cost of changes in the work can, however, have potential disadvantages, because a competent contractor has another method of costing at his disposal. He has, in a running contract, rates and prices available which are of later date than the original tender figures and reflect more accurately the real costs of execution. Also, in controlling the work in progress, he is continually optimising the methods and resources required to complete the remaining work. He does not have to adhere rigidly to his preconceived cost plan, although the performance of the work will no doubt be compared to the prediction. Thus, in planning the work still to be done, he can seek the least-cost solution that is consistent with quality and programme constraints.

The emphasis here is on the remaining work — the costs of the construction already completed cannot be controlled; only the resource costs of the work still to be done can be optimised. This approach is based on real costs and is forward-looking.

The type of contract, therefore, is a fundamental consideration in controlling costs, especially where changes in scope of work, significant in their cost implications, occur during construction. The issue is not just the relative flexibility to accommodate change which is discussed in chapter 5. In addition, only certain types of contracts based on cost-target or cost-reimbursable principles give the Client access to the Contractor's cost optimisation at a given time and a share in any advantage arising from it. What is happening in most types of contract is that the Contractor may alter his detailed methods of working or programme sequence of work because he sees an opportunity to use his resources more efficiently, but he is under no obligation to disclose these details in full.

So, in any particular project, the following questions must be asked.

- What types of contracts are being used?
- Do they suit the work breakdown structure?
- Who is carrying the risks?
- Who is really controlling cost and time at each level?

The last question is especially important in major projects where there is a complex structure of different contracts and work packages.

Communications. In the hurly-burly of a busy project site, clear communication is often difficult, and the consequences of poor communication can be disastrous. The oft-repeated litany of advice to construction teams and managers runs as follows — much simplifed, of course:

- reports must be timely, accurate, factual, concise and distributed to those who need them
- instructions must always be written and accord with set procedures (because memories are short)
- meetings should be sufficient in number but not too many; each must have a specific purpose, the right people present, and a planned agenda circulated beforehand with any documents required for discussion
- minutes should be concise and should record actions taken or required
- important information, which may be exchanged informally or through 'informal links', should be brought formally to the attention of those who need to know, at the first opportunity.

The notion of distinguishing between formal and informal links is very useful in the construction context. In management jargon, 'formal links' means the sort of communications described above: reports, meetings and so on which are part of the contractual or statutory relationships and which become part of the project record. 'Informal links' means the exchange of factual information and opinion between individuals in a responsible fashion to enable them to do their job. This may be on a regular or *ad hoc* basis, depending on the needs of the project.

For the success of projects, large or small, good communications are essential. They depend on the ability to keep issues simple and to get to the core of a problem — and on knowing how to ask the right questions when necessary.

7.3 Review topics

Procurement

Procurement of materials and equipment may be executed separately from the construction contracts, particularly for large or complex projects. In such situations, a procurement group should be organised to execute the work, usually as part of the project management team.

A review of the procurement system should consider questions such as the following.

- How is the procurement group organised? What are its responsibilities? Is it operating effectively?
- Have standard procedures for the whole procurement cycle been written and disseminated? Are they being followed?
- Do the supply packages accord with the WBS? Do the terms and conditions fully complement those in the construction contracts?
- Are effective measures in force for planning, scheduling and expediting of supplies?
- Have the time schedule, cost budget and purchase conditions for each item been defined?
- Are the tender evaluation procedures satisfactory?
- Are effective procedures in force for ensuring that necessary approvals are obtained before a purchases order is committed or issued?
- Has the quality control plan been prepared in detail? Does it regulate quality control and inspection effectively?
- Have external inspection agencies been appointed (as necessary)

and briefed? Are they operating in accordance with the quality control plan?

- Have standards been defined for documentation required from suppliers? Are they being followed? (Note — documents include design data, materials certification, commissioning details, and operation and maintenance manuals.)

Construction

The construction phase represents the commitment of most of the project expenditure. A review of the construction phase should consider questions such as the following.

- Have the types of contract and work packaging been selected to accord with the project objectives?
- Do the contracts clearly define the Contractor's areas of work and responsibilities related to site management?
- Are all necessary functions represented at the site? Who is responsible for each?
- Are the various organisations at site adequately staffed? Are the responsibilities of individual managers clear, and their interfaces defined and understood?
- Is the detailed design complete? What parts of it remain to be done? Is the management of the design/construction interface effective?
- What risks or uncertainties are present in this phase? Which party is carrying the risks?
- How are time and cost contingencies managed? Is an effective procedure for change order control being used?
- Have the methods and sequence of construction been defined and agreed?
- Is there an effective quality plan? Is it being followed?
- Have all the necessary statutory approvals been obtained?
- Have the basic contractual requirements of insurances and health and safety at site (and compliance of subcontractors with such requirements) been properly thought through and implemented?
- Are the responsibilities and functions of site office and head office well defined and linked? (This may apply to both Client and Contractors.)
- Are the reporting systems producing the correct information as required?

8 Commissioning and start-up

8.1 Introduction

Commissioning is the orderly sequence of testing, adjustment and bringing into operation of those subunits and units of the project, after the construction and installation work is finished. The term is most usually applied to dynamic plant, i.e. projects containing mechanical and electrical equipment and systems whose performance has to be proved under operating conditions.

For relatively simple systems, the commissioning can be straightforward, often following standard procedures and documentation provided by suppliers or published by the appropriate technical authorities. The commissioning of such a system is usually carried out by the Contractor, followed by testing in the presence of the Client's representatives before the project is handed over for use.

The commissioning of a major project is, however, a complex and intricate series of start-up operations and may extend over many months. It requires extensive planning and preparatory work, which commences long before the construction is complete. In such a situation, the user or Client may simply be an observer to the commissioning phase or, depending on the contractual relationships, may take responsibility for it, with the contractors in attendance. In any case, the Client, user and project management should be involved in the planning and preparation for commissioning. Great flexibility is needed in the resourcing of commissioning operations in order to respond to changing circumstances as the work proceeds. In addition, the user should arrange training of operating staff sufficiently in advance for them to participate in commissioning and start-up.

119

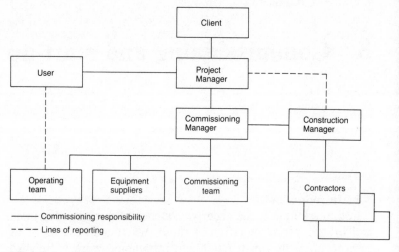

Fig. 8.1. Typical commissioning management organisation

8.2 Commissioning organisation

Whatever the contractual relationships, the commissioning of a major project involves a number of parties and needs active management. The management organisation for both precommissioning and commissioning should be agreed and key personnel mobilised during the construction phase. The principal criteria that should be set for the commissioning organisation are as follows:

- a simple structure to suit the specialised nature of the work, i.e. avoiding multiple layers of management
- single point responsibility for all commissioning activities with the appointment of a commissioning manager
- formation of an integrated team, each member having clearly specified responsibilities, authority and resources, while respecting the contractual relationships between the parties involved
- active involvement of the user in the commissioning of the plant.

A typical commissioning management organisation is shown in Fig. 8.1.

8.3 The commissioning process

Whether the project is complex or relatively simple, a number of preconditions for commissioning must be met. It should be recognised that commissioning is not simply an extension of construction, but a separate set of activities which cut across those of supply and construction. The commissioning process must be integrated with construction completion dates and must take into account the construction continuing alongside for some portions of the project. For example, construction proceeds on the basis of physical site areas and technical specialisations, whereas the project is commissioned on the basis of complete units or subsystems. Some equipment items may be installed months ahead of the date when the unit to which they belong is ready for testing. Hence the importance of the commissioning organisation being in place ahead of time, as described in section 8.2, so that the team can participate in the preparatory work.

The preparations required ahead of commissioning can be described under the following headings:

- the commissioning schedule
- the commissioning programme
- general requirements
- staffing and training schedule for commissioning/operating staff
- documentation.

The commissioning schedule

The schedule should list all the items to be commissioned and their interdependence. Frequently, five levels of progressive commissioning need to be recognised (or more for complex projects). These levels are:

- subunits — individual plant and equipment items
- units — groups of equipment forming an operating unit
- subsystems — complete production or service units with their instrumentation and controls, together with fire protection and damage warning and security systems
- systems — all subsystems in combination, with system-level controls
- the project — the whole project as an operating establishment.

There should also be contingency plans to permit alternative commissioning sequences, if required.

The commissioning programme

Various tests must be undertaken and commissioning points achieved at each of the five levels. A project commissioning programme is therefore required, supported by detailed programmes at each level. These programmes must take account of and show explicitly two factors of fundamental importance:

- the criticality of each commissioning operation
- contingency plans to overcome delays in commissioning individual units/subsystems.

The commissioning activities may include the following:

- unit tests (e.g. rotating or moving machines)
- dry runs
- operational testing at subsystem level
- production runs
- commissioning of subsystems
- simulation of malfunction
  - o operation of control and safety interlocks
  - o operation of standby subsystems
  - o operation of emergency subsystems (uninterruptable power supplies, fire protection, damage warning etc.)
- tests of maintainability
- preparation of snagging lists, and action on them
- post-commissioning tests.

The last item relates to tests that can be made only after the system has been put into operation, e.g. full-load, performance or production capacity tests.

General requirements

- Specification of performance and of the required supplier's documentation
- definition and agreement of responsibility for each activity in the programme
- arrangements and facilities for the attendance, when required, of project staff, operations staff, contractors' and suppliers' representatives, specialists, statutory undertakings and other supervisory personnel
- supplies of power, water, etc. to be available for test purposes

when required, including temporary arrangements if necessary
- materials for commissioning, including consumables and spares
- labour for commissioning
- spares for operation
- plans and procedures for rectifying defects
- plans for support during post-commissioning period.

Staffing and training arrangements

As staff, particularly supervisory staff, may be brought together from various sources into the commissioning teams, their training individually and as a team must be planned and completed. The user's staff who will operate the project when it is completed should also be available at the start of commissioning, or even earlier. If they are to be effective during commissioning, their training must be completed in advance of the requirement.

Although the timing and details of training vary widely between projects, the critical issue is as always that fully trained competent operating teams must be deployed at the right time to ensure that the project is commissioned and put into operation quickly and efficiently.

Documentation

Commissioning is the focal point for the finalisation of project documentation. There are three categories of documents: those to be handed over by contractors, those needed to commission the project successfully, and those required for operation and maintenance by the user. The generating, expediting, collating and issue of each of these is a special task which needs to be organised. Examples of the documents required are listed below — some are needed for commissioning, such as certificates of insurance, permits, drawings, operation and maintenance manuals:

- certificates of insurance — of the works and of persons, during both commissioning and operation
- permits for operation of the project, connection and use of external power and water, pressure vessels, discharge of effluents, etc.
- test certificates at all levels

  o of materials and components
  o of completion of installation

- o of readiness for commissioning
- o results of safety checks and studies of hazardous operations
- o final quality assurance report
- design and performance specifications
- full as-constructed drawings
- records of defects and deficiencies, action taken and retesting, with an analysis of consequential delays and their causes
- certificates of complete commissioning
- operation and maintenance manuals
- plans and procedures for decommissioning
- certificate of project hand-over
- snagging list of outstanding work requiring attention post-commissioning.

Almost all of the above are, or should be, provided to the Client and the user in support of the project hand-over, as evidence that the project is complete in all respects and fit for safe operation.

8.4 Review topics

The foregoing discussion highlights certain general questions that a review of commissioning arrangements should consider, as follows.

- Have the units, the subsystems and the whole system to be commissioned been defined?
- Has the scope of commissioning work been established? Are effective procedures for its execution laid down, including performance specifications and contractual definition of required suppliers' documentation?
- Has a realistic programme been prepared and agreed? Is the planned end date for commissioning co-ordinated with achievable dates for the completion of construction?
- Is the commissioning programme integrated with on-going construction work and partial operation?
- Have the necessary permits been obtained?
- Are arrangements for insurances and for safety at site during commissioning satisfactory?
- Have emergency procedures and individual responsibilities for their implementation been established?
- Have the points where management responsibility passes from construction to the commissioning organisation been defined,

together with transfer and exchange of supporting documentation?

- Are there adequate arrangements for power and water supplies for commissioning, and for the attendance of statutory undertakings?
- Are there adequate arrangements for the attendance of suppliers' representatives and other external specialists, and for participation of operations staff?
- Have materials, consumables and spares for commissioning been obtained?
- Are contracts agreed for the supply of commissioning labour?
- Are appropriate resources available for rectifying defects and deficiencies and for evaluating their effects on the programme?
- Are the methods of controlling and reporting progress effective? How are check lists of outstanding work being prepared and are they being followed up?
- Are there effective procedures for the transition from commissioning to project hand-over?
- Have proper arrangements been made for the production and issue of the hand-over documentation? Is the documentation complete and of the required quality?
- Have satisfactory arrangements been made for ensuring completion of contractual obligations, including provision of operational spares, rectification of snagging lists, support to the user during the post-commissioning period, and conducting and attending any further tests required?

The commissioning phase is the last link in the long chain of completing a project. It could also be described as the first step towards generation of a positive cash flow, and on that account its importance should not be underestimated, either in time or money terms.

9 Project performance review

9.1 Introduction

Capital investment projects should be subject to the same regular checks, tight control and accountability as any other business. Good management, clear procedures and controls are essential if the Client's time, cost, quality and performance objectives are to be achieved. In practice, however, managements tend to underestimate the commercial and technical requirements, and frequently run projects without adequate checks on performance. A history of spectacular failures of projects has resulted, in both the public and private sectors.

Whether the investment is in a new manufacturing plant, a sophisticated computer system or an expressway, the success of the project depends on good project management based on a well conceived strategic plan and an effective project organisation. In this chapter the reasons for project failure are discussed, indicating where a project performance review can help to account for and reduce the risks involved. The methods used in a review are described, and some typical problems encountered are discussed. Finally, benefits to the Client from regular project performance reviews are outlined.

Many project managers do not recognise sufficiently that management should be open rather than secretive, always excepting the demands of inherent confidentiality. Others believe, perhaps more wisely, that no Project Manager and no system is infallible and that the informed opinion of fresh minds at crucial times of review is often of great benefit. An independent review, properly constituted, represents neither a loss of control nor an admission of failure. In many cases it is the Project Managers who gain immediate benefit from requesting such a review.

9.2 Project failures

Frequently, projects run into trouble and show problems of delay, overspending or failure to satisfy the user's needs. While the causes of these problems are various, some combination of the following factors is usually involved.

- The project was badly conceived, without sufficient forethought or examination of the internal and external factors that might affect it.
- The scope of the work was not adequately defined and agreed by the participants. In some cases the end user's expectations were not satisfied because they were unrealistic and changed during the life of the project.
- The user was often kept at arm's length from the development of the project — as a result, his requirements were inadequately specified at an early stage and he was not involved in approvals of choice vital to his needs.
- Conflicting objectives and requirements of the various organisations involved had not been identified.
- The project was badly organised, with poor channels of communication and control systems and possibly lack of motivation; this resulted in confused understanding of responsibilities within the project team.
- The amount of planning was inappropriate to the scale of the project; stages were not clearly identified with agreed deliverables.
- Optimistic planning led to an underestimation of resources which inevitably resulted in inefficiency and delay.
- The risks associated with the project were not identified, and action was not taken to transfer or make contingency for these risks.
- Consideration of an appropriate contract strategy was left until late in the project, when the full range of options was no longer available to the Client.
- Change order control was poor, resulting in cost growth during the development of the project.

The most common single cause of project failure is an inappropriate project organisation, having the wrong people in key positions with their roles and responsibilities being neither well defined nor understood.

In such situations, the advantages to be gained in the project from a well-conceived independent review have become widely recognised. To be well-conceived, the review should be timely, concentrate on the key issues associated with the project, identify weaknesses and recommend improvements to protect the promoter's interests. Project performance reviews have been developed to satisfy this requirement.

9.3 Project performance reviews

A project performance review is a formal and systematic technical, financial and managerial review of a project. It is carried out by experienced specialists at any stage in the project, with the following aims:

- to determine whether the current and proposed project organisation is right for the task
- to evaluate the approach adopted by the project team to setting and implementing objectives
- to verify the progress achieved to date against the plan
- to examine the effects of financial, material, manpower and other restraints on progress
- to recommend, if appropriate, the changes necessary to improve performance.

The project reviewer should investigate the underlying project records, the tangible results of work done, and the project organisation and managment, as well as the systems and controls in place. This enables the reviewer to report under five headings, as follows.

- The current status of the project at the time of the audit as compared with the project objectives
- the forecast result of the project as compared with project objectives
- management issues that may affect the successful completion of the project
- risks associated with the project
- lessons that can be usefully applied to other projects.

A project performance review is an activity of measurement against predefined and relevant standards. To achieve results that are independent of the individual project reviewer's biases, the review must be conducted according to established methods and be subject to formal principles. These methods and principles must be accepted by those who commission project performance reviews and by the project teams whose work is to be studied. Naturally, in executing a review, the reviewer(s) must exercise personal judgement; but the adoption of standards of measurement should ensure objectivity and prevent the review report from emerging merely as an expression of personal opinion.

A project performance review is designed to be a practical, cost effective and independent source of information about a project. It is intended to serve as a support to and a basis for management decision-making, and should therefore make recommendations, but the responsibility for making decisions should remain with the project management.

The information presented in the project reviewer's report must be reliable, result directly from an examination and analysis of appropriate data, and be presented in a form directly usable by management for making decisions. One of the aims of the report is to reduce uncertainty about the project as far as possible. Where uncertainties remain the report should identify them, and emphasise and examine the significant ones.

As a project performance review is concerned with the Client's exposure to risks and potential losses, it should be accepted as a critical activity. It should identify actual and potential deficiencies related to the project's execution and the means to correct them. It is less concerned with identifying and reporting exceptional strengths and accomplishments. The results must nevertheless be credible to those concerned: not only must the report be objective and fair but also the review itself must be conducted openly with full consultation and it must be visible to the responsible management throughout.

9.4   Project review methodology
Figure 9.1 is a flow chart summarising the approach to a project performance review.

Selection of the review team
However specific the call for help from a project, the review team should always be prepared to find a situation very different from that defined. If the solution were easily seen, no help would be

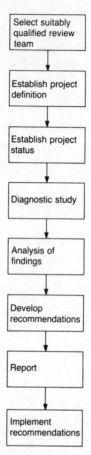

Fig. 9.1. Project performance review: flow chart

needed. Thus, flexibility of approach to the review is a factor in selecting the combination of experience and skills which will compose the review team. It should also be remembered that in remote locations access to specialists may not be available.

The success of a project performance review relies to a large extent on the review team gaining the support and respect of the members of the Client's project team, particularly during the diagnostic stage. The review team must be objective and open-minded in the pursuit of their enquiries, and must be prepared to overcome the natural suspicions, or hostility, of some members of the Client's project team, particularly if problems are being encountered in their areas of responsibility.

The essential attributes of each member of the review team are as follows:

- the experience and personality to obtain the confidence of and establish a rapport with members of the Client's project team at all levels
- competence to understand the relevant technology
- the skill to obtain and assimilate all relevant information quickly and tactfully, bearing in mind that much of it will be gained from discussions with competent and busy people
- the ability to identify and evaluate problems and their causes and to propose remedial action.

Project definition

The review team must establish and understand the basic parameters governing the project. These include the project objectives, scope and standard of work, key programme dates and cost budget limits.

Project status

The present status of the project should be reviewed to establish the divergences between the requirements stated in the project definition and the probable effects on the final outcome. Where realistic planning and control procedures have not been established, a time schedule and cash flow may have to be produced by the review team as a basis for the appraisal.

Diagnostic study

The central activity in a project performance review is the diagnostic study. This should be planned to reveal the problems underlying any shortfall in the technical, programme, budget, financial, contractual, organisational, management, communications, control and political aspects of the project.

While comparison of the present project status with the project definition will reveal the principal causes of difficulty, the project review must also examine and keep under question all aspects of project activity. Experience has shown that an identified problem may be linked with other, unsuspected deficiencies; each of these may contribute, but there is usually no sole reason for the overall status of the project.

A broad but searching investigation should therefore be undertaken before concentrating in detail on the specific problem areas. This close examination of these aspects and their interrelationships can be achieved by working to a planned check list.

A diagnostic study will usually be based on interviews with individual members of the Client's project team, together with an analysis of the projects's documentation and control procedures covering project manuals, project plans, programmes, progress reports, budgets, cost reports, financial reports, contract documents, correspondence memoranda, minutes of meetings etc. During this fact-finding stage, the co-operation of the members of the Client's project team is essential. They should be consulted and their experience utilised as much as possible.

The review team should encourage the Client's project team to propose and discuss with them their own ideas on solutions and possible alternatives. Their contributions to the final recommended actions can be invaluable. The discussions often also reveal unexpected opinions, which may prepare the ground for the acceptance of the report and the implementation of the solutions put forward.

Evaluation of findings

Members of the review team should meet regularly during the diagnostic study to compare their findings, reveal interlinked problems, and decide the direction and emphasis of further investigations. The need for clarifications or additional information may arise and instigate a second round of interviews; these should be allowed for in the planning of the interview programme for the review.

On completion of the diagnostic study, the review team should make a combined evaluation of their findings to identify the extent and effect of all deficiencies in the performance of the project and their real causes.

A verbal presentation of the findings of the diagnostic study to the senior management of the project can be valuable. The response of this audience helps to confirm the preliminary findings of the review team, and frequently reveals any misunderstandings.

Recommendations

The review team should recommend a plan of corrective action. These recommendations must be practical, objective, and derived from the diagnostic study and the verbal presentation.

If the problems are identified sufficiently early in the project's development, the actions recommended may create a turnround in the project performance to achieve the planned objectives. On the other hand, if the audit takes place in the later stages, it may only be possible to obviate the occurrence of future problems and to stabilise adverse trends.

Reports

Project performance reviews usually conclude with the preparation of a confidential written report to the Client. This should concentrate on the main issues and recommend specific and practical project actions. It should also include all the relevant supporting facts, figures, opinions and conclusions arising from the review.

Implementation of recommendations

Successful project performance reviews should result in the prompt implementation of the recommendations within a defined timescale with the support of the project team. These recommendations are normally based on the review team's own experience, but innovative ideas can also prove acceptable if they are practical and appropriate.

Retention of the review team to assist or advise in the implementation phase of the report's recommendations is advantageous. Once these recommendations are introduced and seen to be implemented and effective, the review team should be withdrawn.

9.5 Benefits of a project performance review

A project performance review will provide the Client with:

- a review by an independent party with no position to defend
- a status report on the performance of the project, in which problems, key issues and their effect on the project are identified
- practical recommendations for the improvement of project performance.

133

The specific benefits of a project performance review depend largely on the perspective of the individual organisation and its role in the project, but it should enable the Client to:

- anticipate problems rather than react to them
- manage risks and problems so as to reduce or eliminate their impact
- evaluate opportunities to increase or decrease participation in the project
- gain an independent view of the performance of the project team in contributing to the project's success
- confirm that the user's requirements are well understood, defined and achievable within the restraints imposed on the project
- be reassured that effective planning and cost control methods are being used on the project.

Frequently, an important benefit arises from the act of the review itself. People involved in the project and in full flight are required to pause to take stock of where they are and where they are going; this can be very valuable. The probing questions of the project review team provide a new perspective and an opportunity for those in the project organisation to reconsider their established thinking.

Appendix A   Project viability

A.1   Introduction

This appendix deals with procedures for evaluating project cash flows before financing, concentrating mainly on the use and interpretation of internal rates of return, but mentioning other useful techniques. It relates to section 4.4, and comprises additional information about the methods of project evaluation described therein. The methods are used in the feasbility phase but may be employed at any time that an assessment of financial or economic viability is required.

A.2   Definitions

Project viability. For present purposes this general term means the ability of a project to meet predetermined objectives, which may be technical, economic, social, financial, or all of these.

Financial viability. A project can be said to be financially viable if it meets the objectives of profitability by acceptable means; financial viability thus relates to a number of criteria in combination, including profitability, limitation of investment, restraints on cash flow and timing (see section 4.1).

Economic viability. The ability of a project to meet economic objectives.

Net cash flow (NCF). The difference between revenue accruing to the project and cash outflows, both calculated on an annual basis.

Discounted cash flow (DCF). See section A.4.

Net present value (NPV). The value of the net cash flow (or net benefit stream) when discounted over time to a base year, usually the first year of construction or operation (see section A.5).

Internal rate of return (IRR). The annual discount rate which when applied to the cash flows yields an NPV of zero.

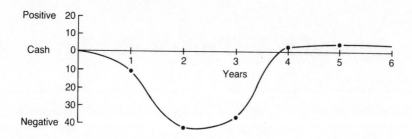

Fig. A.1. Net cash flow

Return to equity. A special calculation of the IRR to the equity holders (i.e. the shareholders in a business).

Benefit. A revenue or other cash inflow, calculated in economic terms.

First year rate of return. A measure that compares the benefit in the first year of operation with the capital cost of the project.

Cost/benefit ratio. The ratio between the values of the discounted cost and benefit streams.

NPV/cost ratio. A measure of net benefit compared with the accompanying costs.

Payback period. The number of years required before a positive return is gained on the original investment.

Economic opportunity cost. An economic term meaning the cost of a resource as measured by its value in alternative uses — usually excludes taxes, subsidies and transfer payments.

cif. The cost of imported materials or equipment, including the supplier's price plus carriage, insurance and freight charges. (Note: the cost of the equipment delivered to the works site would include other items over and above the cif cost, such as custom duties, warehousing and transport from the port to the work site.)

A.3 Objectives and methodology
The cash flow table

The start of the evaluation procedure is a net cash flow for each year of the project throughout the project life. The elements of this cash flow are shown in the following example, in which the flow of capital investment becomes 'fixed assets'. As the example is an industrial facility, the user would normally incur other

Table 1. Cash flow table for first 4 years: £ m (without inflation), brackets signify negative value

Years	1	2	3	4
Cash outflows				
Fixed assets	10	40	30	—
Other preproduction costs	1	2	5	—
Operating costs	—	—	2	6
Working capital	—	—	3	2
Subtotal	11	42	40	8
Revenues	—	—	3	10
Net cash flow	(11)	(42)	(37)	2

expenditures in preparing for production, hence these are termed 'other preproduction costs' (see Table 1).

The intention is to decide whether or not the later positive cash flows are sufficient to offset the effects of the earlier negative cash flows.

Methods of approach

The project can be viewed in several ways. If comparisons are to be made between projects, the same standpoint must be adopted for each, as follows.

Project standpoint. The basic financial assessment is made from this standpoint. The project is regarded as an activity on its own. Costs, revenues and cash flows are calculated before allowing for financing charges at commercial rates. Normally everyone concerned is interested in this evaluation.

National/regional standpoint. From this viewpoint the economic assessment is produced. Governments will be interested in the contribution of the project to the public good, especially in developing countries, as will international funding agencies if they are involved. Commercial bodies are more interested in this type of analysis than they used to be, because of environmental awareness.

Enterprise standpoint. Companies will be especially interested in the effects of the project on the return to equity (the owners') and potential sources of finance will want to see how funds are to be made up and how safe their position is.

The cash flow forms the starting point for both of the financial assessments (including and excluding financing charges).

A.4 Discounted cash flow
Project life

The net cash flow must be set out for a reasonable period of time — most problems in engineering economics involve determining what is economical in the long run. The project life is rarely under 5 years; usually it is 15–20 years. In such problems it is necessary to recognise the time value of money. Money can earn interest, so £1 now is worth more than £1 in a year's time.

The DCF techniques recognise this and compare the investment cash outflow with the operating cash inflow over a period of time. Project life is commonly 15 years for a medium size manufacturing project or a technology with limited life, and 20 years for a larger project or more stable technology. Sometimes small projects or improvement schemes are evaluated over a life of only 5–10 years. Project life should not be excessively long. The longer the life, the higher the DCF performance.

Discounting

The general case for the present value of a future cash flow is given by a variation of the compound interest formula:

$$\text{Present value} = \sum_{i=0}^{n} \frac{C_i}{(1+r)^i}$$

where r is the interest rate per period, n is the number of periods and C_i is the cash flow in period i. When r, the interest rate or 'discount' rate is 10% the factor for next year is $1/(1 + 0 \cdot 1)$, i.e. $0 \cdot 909$, and for the year after it is $1/(1 + 0 \cdot 1)^2$, i.e. $0 \cdot 826$. Computer software is available to handle the DCF calculations and produce the NPV, IRR or other required results.

A.5 Net present value and internal rate of return

The DCF technique can be used to evaluate a project in two ways, or variations of them.

● The NPV of all the cash flows can be calculated — this is the

138

present value of all future earnings or savings over the project life minus the present value of the investment. To caculate NPV a discount rate must be selected.

- The IRR can be calculated. This is the annual interest rate or rate of discount which when applied to the cash flows will produce a net present value of zero. It is the true annual rate of return on the outstanding capital investment.

Net present value

The procedure for calculating NPV is illustrated below in the case of a labour saving machine costing £1 m and saving £0·1 m/year. A conservative estimate of project life of only 5 years is chosen. As the machine still has usefulness at the end of the period, a residual value is credited to the cash flow, as shown in Table 2.

Net present value is 1·160−0·888, i.e. £0·272 m.

Assuming the choice to be between simply installing the machine and investing the money somewhere else at an interest rate of 10%, the business would be £0·27 m better off in present value by installing the machine.

Some firms prefer to show the relationship between present values out and in as a ratio; thus 1·160/0·888 = £1·306 m.

Internal rate of return

From the previous example it is clear that the investment is earning at a rate greater than 10%. If the cash flow is discounted

Table 2.   Procedure for calculating NPV: £ m

	Cash Flow		Discount factor 10%	Present value	
Year	Out	In		Out	In
0	1·0	—	1·00	1·000	—
1		0·1	0·91	—	0·091
2		0·3	0·83	—	0·249
3		0·4	0·75	—	0·300
4		0·4	0·68	—	0·272
5		0·4	0·62	—	0·248
6	(0·2)	—	0·56	(0·112)	—
				0·888	1·160

at 18% the NPV becomes zero; thus, the true annual rate of return is 18%.

To determine this IRR it is necessary to calculate the NPV at different discount rates and then interpolate between them to find zero NPV (the relationship between discount factor and NPV is not linear, so the chosen points for interpolation should not be too far apart).

NPV or IRR?

Both methods have their advantages, but the information they provide about the project value is different. For example, a very high IRR on a small investment will still produce a large NPV. The main objective is sometimes to maximise the NPV or the NPV/cost ratio, depending on circumstances; where more than one project is being examined both must be considered.

The same cash flow data are used to derive both the NPV and the IRR. Often both indices are presented — in practice, however, the business analyst makes more use of the IRR because he has worked with the data and knows the scale of the project.

Acceptable IRR

Some businesses use a minimum IRR — this depends on the inherent profitability and stability of the enterprise. It is usually possible to obtain a real return of up to 5% tax free from safe investment in financial markets. Commercial enterprises will therefore normally be seeking an IRR of 10% or better from their investments. Small projects, especially those which have not received, or cannot justify, extensive evaluation are sometimes subject to a cut-off rate of 15% or more. Projects with lower rates are rejected. Analysts should beware of specified cut-off rates unless these are the result of a careful study of the requirements of the business and its opportunities. Individual projects need to be evaluated in the light of alternative opportunity.

There is a strong tendency for IRR to decrease with successive stages of project evaluation, as initially optimistic cash flow estimates become more realistic. The analyst should beware of high IRRs unless the benefits flow partly from making extra use of existing facilities (e.g. some rehabilitation or improvement projects).

Selection of the discount factor

The discount factor applied to the cash flow is usually related in some way to the cost of capital. If the enterprise is financed, say, half by loans with a real interest rate of 5% and half by equity accustomed to receiving a pretax return of 15%, then it would be realistic to discount the cash flows at the mean of these two rates, say 10%. A project with a positive NPV at this discount rate (or an IRR above 10%) is likely to enhance overall performance.

So far, the evaluation should be conducted in terms of constant prices (without inflation). But the future flows of costs and revenues will be subject to inflation; hence a further calculation of cash flow profiles must be made to include its effects. These cash flows are said to be expressed in money or current price terms. In this case, the real return can be calculated by dividing the inflated return by the inflation rate. A 10% return with 5% inflation is a real return of $1 \cdot 1/1 \cdot 05 = 1 \cdot 048$, i.e. 4.8%.

In the absence of financial or other guidelines, it is usual to use a discount factor of $\sim 10\%$. A factor can also be selected based on the opportunity cost of capital, i.e. what could be earned by investing the funds elsewhere, for example in other projects or in government stock. The UK Government Treasury 'test discount rate' for public sector projects is 5% in real terms.

Project risk should not be taken into account in selecting the discount factor (but a market risk factor is reflected in the cost of equity capital). Risk is allowed for through sensitivity or risk analysis.

It should be remembered that when the discount factor is varied this alters the NPV and can alter the ranking of competing projects. When calculating an IRR it is not necessary to select a discount factor, although the IRR still has to be compared with a target rate in order to interpret the result.

Comprehensive cost

It is conventional to use IRR and NPV as appraisal tools. Another method of DCF approach, rarely used but very useful, is 'comprehensive costing'. The irregular investment that precedes operation or use of the asset can be converted into an equal annual charge throughout the life of the project. This annual charge can be added to the annual operating cost to give a total annual cost, which can then be roughly compared with annual revenue.

Alternatively, both costs and revenues can be expressed in relation to a unit of production.

In essence, the procedure involves making the present value of the investment equal to the present value of the operating surplus needed to remunerate the investment. It can be used effectively to compare options with similar implementation programmes but different levels of investment.

A.6 Other DCF approaches

Only cash flows before financing have been considered in the above analysis. It is possible to prepare a schedule of cash flows to equity after financing — in this case, instead of setting out the actual investment, the analyst sets out the schedule of loan drawings and repayments and the appropriate interest payments. The remaining cash requirement is financed by the owners (shareholders). This is their equity and in future years any surplus cash after paying for operations and meeting the loan obligations is the property of the equity holders. Thus, the IRR to the equity holders can be calculated.

Often the cash flows are prepared after inflation because loan interests are in money values, i.e. subject to inflation. If the real interest rate can be estimated, this can be used and all cash flows will be in real values. The return to equity will be before tax. If the tax liability is known, this can be included in the cash flows. Sometimes tax effects influence project viability significantly, e.g. tax holidays. In this case an after-tax evaluation is necessary. But tax liability is usually a complicated calculation, and the analyses are often prepared on the basis of pretax returns.

A.7 Economic assessment

The economic assessment is concerned with the worth of the project to the community as well as the developer or user. The worth to the community is measured as the net resource cost savings (or benefits) deriving from the project (see section 4.4).

The requirement for economic evaluation arises because in many countries, including to some extent developing countries, the market prices have been affected by price subsidies, protective tariffs, monopolistic powers or other distortions. The price of an article may be artificially high within a country, but what would it fetch on the export market? A public sector company may pay a good wage to its unskilled labour, but would they be able to earn the same wage in the private sector? Any such differences must be taken into account, so that the prices used reflect the economic cost of resources accurately.

The capital and maintenance and operating costs of the project should be calculated in constant price terms throughout an assumed lifetime of the project, thus producing a profile of costs against time. DCF techniques should then be employed to compare the profile of costs with the corresponding stream of 'resource cost benefits'.

The types of benefits to be taken into account are listed below, using a road scheme as an example. It will be noted that double counting could easily distort the calculations; care is always needed to avoid this pitfall (section 4.4). Typical benefits are:

- savings in materials and energy
- savings in time
- savings in accidents/damage etc.
- improved health and welfare
- improved productivity
- generated agricultural and industrial output
- changes in land use and land values.

The net resource cost benefits are the difference between the two DCF streams, i.e. the benefits minus the costs. The results, for each option, can be expressed in the following forms:

- NPV
- IRR
- first year rate of return
- cost/benefit ratio
- NPV/cost ratio
- payback period.

In arriving at the NPV of an option, various discount rates can be used; frequently, however, the rate adopted is the prevailing test discount rate (TDR) as recommended by the UK Treasury, or (overseas) rates suggested by central authorities to suit the social opportunity cost of capital in the country concerned. In broad terms, projects with a positive NPV will show an IRR above the TDR and should therefore be worth considering further. The NPV is generally regarded as the measure that best reflects the worth

143

to the community—a high NPV represents favourable assessment.

The economic IRR is not generally used in public sector projects but, being analogus to the IRR of financial assessment, it has its place in private sector applications. The first year rate of return is not widely used as a measure of viability, but is useful in considering how the timing of a project may affect the economic return. The payback period is used as a supplementary indicator only.

As mentioned above, the prices used should reflect the economic cost of resources accurately. These are the prices which result when all the distortions (subsidies, etc.) have been removed. The technique, sometimes called shadow pricing, involves valuing items in terms of their economic opportunity costs — their value in alternative uses, taking international costs into account where appropriate. The issues are complex, and engender differences of opinion between economists. The principal adjustments incorporated in World Bank or UNIDO procedures are as follows.

- Import duties on capital goods and materials are excluded, as are internal transfers such as domestic taxes — these do not represent use of resources.
- Production is valued at the price of the alternative supply, i.e. cif imports.
- A shadow price is charged for labour.
- All goods supplied locally and consumed in the business which could be traded internationally are subject to a price adjustment (in the World Bank method).
- Where the exchange rate is regarded as being artificial (the local currency is probably overvalued) a premium may be added to all valuations made at cif import prices. This places extra value on foreign exchange savings and extra penalties on foreign exchange use (in the UNIDO method).

The usual effect of such adjustments is to alter the structure of costs and benefits so that the project becomes more attractive, i.e. the economic IRR is higher than the financial IRR. Occasionally, however, the reverse is true.

Projects for public infrastructure are among those whose effective service life may exceed the period of evaluation usually adopted (20 years, say). If the difference is substantial, the benefits which would accrue in the remaining (unexpired) years of the service life should be taken into account. The method is to calculate a residential value and add it to the end of the benefits stream, using the DCF value.

When foreign exchange forms a significant portion of revenues or costs, it is advisable to determine the project foreign exchange rate, known as the 'domestic resource cost' to economists. This rate is the number of units of domestic resource put into the project to save one unit of foreign exchange. The project is attractive, in terms of foreign exchange, when this rate is more favourable than the official currency exchange rate.

In some cases, benefits may be difficult to quantify. The need for the project may then be determined on policy, social or environmental grounds and the aim of the economic analysis would be to find the most cost-effective way of achieving the objective. Here, DCF techniques may be applied to the costs (not the benefits) so as to rank the options in order of 'least cost'. However, the fact that a particular option has the lowest net present cost may not justify its selection; other factors to be considered include the trade-off between cost minimisation and quality of service, the meeting of social aims, comparison between capital and operating cost levels, and so on.

Economic benefits which may enter and may not easily be valued in money terms include:

- generation of employment, both direct and in associated or dependent activities
- generation of incomes locally
- stimulation of economic activity
- savings in foreign exchange, import substitution, impact on balance of payments.

The project may also provide an opportunity for investment elsewhere in the economy, which might be needed to enable its potential benefits to be fully realised.

The technique of quantifying all the factors, including those not easily valued in money terms, is called 'social benefit–cost analysis'. It can be used in a variety of situations, including purely service-giving projects such as highways. Although this is in the domain of economists nowadays, the first practical applications were introduced by engineers in the 1930s when examining the social value of water resources developments in the USA.

145

Finally, the economic assessment should be extended to include sensitivity analysis, as in the case of financial assessment.

A.8 Sensitivity analysis

Sensitivity analysis is discussed as part of risk analysis in section 4.5. The analysis should be applied to both the financial and the economic assessments so as to yield a measure of the robustness of the results for each option under changing conditions. The following notes underline a few points concerning the use of the technique.

The variables which the analyst should examine are:

- changes in the market — including sales opportunity, sale price of products
- changes in input costs — including unit costs of materials, labour costs
- inability of management to operate as planned — including delay in achieving full production
- serious overrun in capital cost or construction period — including funding interest rate capital cost, delay in commissioning.

Revenues are usually a critical variable on commercial projects. The analyst should first present the variables and the changes in them that would render the option non-viable. These can be shown in a table on the lines of that shown in the main text (p. 53). A simple graph may be helpful in supporting the table, such as that shown in Fig. A.2.

This graph, based on a sensitivity calcuation, shows how the IRR for an option (the NPV could similarly be used) would be affected by changes in revenues and capital cost respectively. The starting point for the graph is the result of the assessment of an option; it is assumed that the result yielded an IRR of 10%. The y-axis in this case shows the actual percentage IRR, i.e. 'y% return on investment'. The x-axis represents the percentage *change* in a variable from a base value. Taking revenue, for example, the base value would be the total revenue used in the original assessment; this is represented by $x = 0$. It appears from the graph that a reduction in revenue of $\sim 13\%$ would reduce the IRR to zero. Such a result is easily calculated on the computer, and indeed is not very onerous or lengthy to perform manually using the DCF assessments already available.

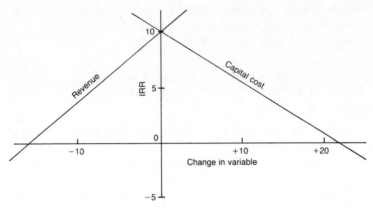

Fig. A.2.   Sensitivity

Similarly, the line showing the influence of capital cost can be calculated and drawn; in this case an increase in capital cost of 25% would again reduce the IRR to zero.

Other variables can be represented similarly. It should be noted that some of the variables do not give a straight-line graph, i.e. the function is not necessarily linear. Nevertheless, they are usually drawn as straight lines, as for practical purposes they can be so regarded over the small ranges of values used in sensitivity analysis. As a rough guide, there is a limit of ~ 15% change in any variable; beyond this the analyst's suspicions must be aroused that a single variable cannot be considered in isolation, therefore the whole situation should be reviewed and the cash flows reworked.

The sensitivity analysis on its own is a simple way of asking 'what if?' questions, but is not an analysis of risk. The probability of the revenue falling by, say, 10% is not given, but the decision maker can see what would happen in that event. The sensitivity analysis is designed to calculate the effects of change in only one variable at a time. Using these results the analyst can also study the effects of variables in simple combinations, and in many cases this is sufficient.

If the viablilty of an option is proved sensitive to the changes that have been considered, risk analysis should be employed so that the uncertainties surrounding the estimates of costs and benefits can be taken fully into account. As described in section 4.5, risk analysis should produce probability distributions that can be mathematically aggregated to yield a probability distribution of changes in the NPV or the IRR.

A.9 Some questions for the business analyst

When examining a project proposal these are some of the questions to consider.

- Are all the main elements of the cash flow set out clearly to produce a net cash flow?
- Can the cash flow elements be traced back to more detailed listings in earlier parts of the study?
- Are all the cash flow items calculated on the same basis (i.e. the same basic costs, inflation assumptions, etc)?
- Are any cash flow items missing? (chapters 7 and 8)
- Do all these cash flow items correctly address the matter of uncertainty/confidence in their earlier treatment?
- Is the project life sensible?
- If NPV is presented, on what basis is the discount factor selected?
- What is a sensible target IRR for this kind of project?
- What movements in individual key parameters would render the project non-viable?
- If an economic (regional or national) viewpoint is required, how were shadow prices and costs generated?
- Are the inputs and the outcome of the evaluation credible?

Appendix B   Specimen cash flow tables

Tables 3−5 are given on pages 150−152.

Table 3. Cash flow table (example)

ECU million at end of 1981 values

	1982	1983	1984	1985	1986	1987	1988	1989	1990	1991	1992	1993	1994	1995	1996	1997	1998	1999 and after
Sales revenue		–	–	–	93·5	130·1	133·1	136·2	140·2	175·6	201·2	207·4	214·4	221·6	225·4	225·4	93·5	93·5
Less costs																		
Production	0·2	1·6	5·0	11·3	78·3	97·1	95·4	95·4	98·6	125·3	138·0	138·0	138·0	138·0	138·0	138·0	0·2	0·2
Fixed assets	5·4	97·5	190·5	77·5	24·1	–	–	16·6	81·7	40·9	–	–	–	–	–	–	–	
Working capital		–	–	0·7	14·4	6·5	0·4	0·4	0·3	6·3	4·3	0·7	0·8	0·9	0·4	–	–	
Total	5·6	99·1	195·5	89·5	116·8	103·6	95·8	112·4	180·6	172·5	142·3	138·7	138·8	138·9	138·4	138·0		
Net cash flow	(5·6)	(99·1)	(195·5)	(89·5)	(23·3)	26·5	37·3	23·8	(40·4)	3·1	58·9	68·7	75·6	82·7	87·0	87·4		
Cumulative cash flow	(5·6)	(104·7)	(300·2)	(389·7)	(413·0)	(386·5)	(349·2)	(325·4)	(365·8)	(362·7)	(303·8)	(235·1)	(159·5)	(76·8)	10·2	97·6		

Table 4. Forecast cash flow in money values (example)

							ECU million in money values									
	1982	1983	1984	1985	1986	1987	1988	1989	1990	1991	1992	1993	1994	1995	1996	1997
Foreign revenues	—	—	—	—	16·6	61·4	57·0	50·7	40·4	85·3	111·1	91·5	64·8	27·9	—	—
Costs																
Production	—	0·2	1·0	4·1	66·7	95·6	99·6	105·2	112·5	158·9	188·4	201·6	215·7	230·8	246·9	264·2
Fixed assets	2·9	59·4	136·9	75·9	28·6	—	—	25·7	98·9	55·7	—	—	—	—	—	—
Working capital	—	—	—	0·8	7·3	7·9	(1·2)	(1·5)	(2·4)	8·7	4·5	(3·9)	(5·0)	(6·1)	(5·5)	(2·0)
Total	2·9	59·6	134·9	80·8	102·6	103·5	98·4	129·4	209·0	223·3	192·2	197·7	210·7	224·7	241·4	262·2
Net cash flow	(2·9)	(59·6)	(134·9)	(80·8)	(86·0)	(42·1)	(41·4)	(78·7)	(168·6)	(138·0)	(81·8)	(106·2)	(145·9)	(196·8)	(241·4)	(262·2)
Domestic revenues	—	—	—	—	153·3	192·6	242·3	304·7	388·0	499·5	644·6	832·7	1076·4	1390·9	1710·3	1966·8
Costs																
Production	0·2	1·7	6·0	13·4	58·0	72·5	83·3	98·1	123·3	169·0	211·7	243·5	280·0	322·0	370·3	425·8
Fixed assets	2·8	55·2	116·7	32·3	7·1	—	—	4·9	92·2	47·9	—	—	—	—	—	—
Working capital	—	—	—	0·2	18·8	4·5	4·9	6·1	8·4	12·3	15·4	19·3	25·6	33·9	33·6	25·0
Total	3·0	56·9	116·7	45·9	83·9	77·0	88·2	109·1	223·9	229·2	227·1	262·8	305·6	355·6	403·9	450·8
Net cash flow	(3·0)	(56·9)	(116·7)	(45·9)	69·4	115·6	154·1	195·6	164·1	270·3	417·5	569·9	770·8	1035·0	1306·0	1516·0
Total net cash flow	(5·9)	(116·5)	(204·6)	(126·7)	(16·6)	73·5	112·7	116·9	(4·5)	132·3	335·7	463·7	624·9	838·2	1065·0	1253·8
Cumulative cash flow																
Foreign	(2·9)	(62·5)	(200·4)	(281·2)	(367·2)	(409·3)	(450·7)	(529·4)	(698·0)	(836·0)	(917·8)	(1024·0)	(1169·9)	(1369·9)	(1608·1)	(1870·3)
Domestic	(3·0)	(59·9)	(173·6)	(222·5)	(153·1)	(37·5)	116·6	312·2	476·3	746·6	1164·1	1734·0	2504·8	3539·8	4846·2	6362·2
Total	(5·9)	(122·4)	(327·0)	(503·7)	(446·8)	(334·1)	(217·2)	(221·7)	(89·4)	246·3	710·0	1334·9	2173·1	3238·1	4491·9	5432·1

151

Table 5. *Project source and use of funds (example)*

	1982	1983	1984	1985	1986	1987	1988	1989	1990	1991	1992	1993	1994	1995	1996	1997
								ECU million in money values								
Users of funds																
Fixed assets	5·7	114·6	247·6	108·2	35·7	—	—	30·6	191·1	103·6					—	—
Working capital				1·0	26·1	12·4	3·7	4·6	6·0	21·0	19·9	15·4	20·6	27·8	28·1	23·0
Repayment of export credits																
I					14·8	29·5	29·5	29·5	29·5	26·9	24·4	24·4	24·4	24·4	12·3	—
II											8·8	17·7	17·7	17·7	17·7	16·5
Repayment of loans																
Direct government loan						2·0	2·0	2·0	3·0	3·0	3·0	3·0	3·0	3·0	3·0	3·0
DB loan									2·0	2·0						
Eurocurrency loan									6·3	6·2	6·3	6·2				
Interest payments																
Export credits I			7·4	17·9	27·5	30·8	27·6	24·0	20·4	17·0	13·8	10·8	7·8	4·8	2·5	0·9
II									3·8	11·5	17·9	18·7	16·8	14·6	12·4	10·3
Direct government loan			1·2	2·4	2·4	2·4	2·4	2·4	2·3	2·1	1·8	1·6	1·3	1·1	0·8	0·6
DB loan			0·5	1·1	1·0	0·9	0·7	0·5	0·3	0·1						
Eurocurrency loan					1·5	2·3	3·0	3·0	2·8	2·3						
Taxation											1·5	0·7	0·2			
Cash surplus/(deficit)						5·6	47·5	62·0	21·4	122·0	42·9	121·4	181·0	260·9	364·7	471·0
Total	5·7	114·6	256·7	130·6	109·0	85·9	116·4	158·6	288·9	317·7	355·6	479·1	645·5	866·0	1093·1	1276·8
Source of funds																
Operating surplus	(0·2)	(1·9)	(7·0)	(17·5)	45·2	85·9	116·4	152·1	192·6	256·9	355·6	479·1	645·5	866·0	1093·1	1276·8
Export credits																
I	—	27·7	131·9	74·8	35·2	—	—									
II								6·5	96·3	60·8						
Loans																
Direct government loan			30·0													
DB loan			10·0													
Eurocurrency loan					25·0											
Equity	5·9	88·8	91·8	73·3	3·6											
Total	5·7	114·0	256·7	130·6	109·0	85·9	116·4	158·6	288·9	317·7	355·6	479·1	645·5	866·0	1093·1	1276·8

Appendix C Life cycle costing

The life cycle cost of an asset is defined as the total cost of the asset over its operating life, including initial acquisition costs and subsequent running costs. Life cycle cost techniques assist decision-making on a project by:

- establishing the total cost commitment
- providing a basis for choice between alternative designs or products (which may differ in both capital and operating costs)
- identifying ways in which reductions in operating costs may be achieved.

There is little difference in principle between these techniques and the methods of evaluation of project options described in chapter 4 in the context of feasibility studies. In both cases, the capital costs incurred at the beginning and the current value of operating costs which arise throughout the life of the project are considered in combination. Particular applications call for different treatments and cost factors to be considered. Life cycle costing techniques can be employed at any point in the project or in the life of an asset when renewals, replacements, change of use or operating management are under consideration.

The principal elements of cost which should be taken into account in the case of a building, for example, are:

- site cost
- capital cost
- fitting-out and furniture
- energy cost
- operating and maintenance or replacement costs
- occupancy cost.

These techniques are not new, having been suggested as long ago as the early 1960s.

Some useful references for further information are provided on page 157.

Further reading

General

Gray C. *et al.* International comparison of project organisation structures; use and effectiveness. *Int. J. Project Management*, 1990, Feb.

Harris F. and McCaffer R. *Modern construction management*, 3rd edn. BSP Professional Books, Oxford, 1989.

Centre for Strategic Studies in Construction. *Investing in building 2001*. National Contractors Group Report, University of Reading, 1989.

Cleland D.I. and King W.R. *The project management handbook*. Van Nostrand Rheinhold, Wokingham, 1988.

Stringer J. *Planning and inquiry process*. MPA Technical Paper No. 6, Templeton College, 1988.

Morris P.W.G. Managing project interfaces — key points for project success. In *The project management handbook*, 2nd edn. Cleland D.I. and King W.R. (eds). Van Nostrand Rheinhold, Wokingham, 1988.

Centre for Strategic Studies in Construction. *Building Britain 2001*. National Contractors Group Report, University of Reading, 1988.

Cleland D.I. The cultural ambience of project management — another look. *Project Management J.*, 1988, **19**, No. 3, June.

Mishan E.J. *Cost benefit analysis*. Unwin Hyman, London, 1988.

Lock D. *The project management handbook*. Gower, Aldershot, 1987.

Morris P.W.G. and Hough G.H. *The anatomy of major projects*. Wiley, Chichester, 1987.

Tatum C.B. The project manager's role in integration design and construction. *Project Management J.*, 1987, **18**, No. 2, June.

Gobeli D.H. and Larson E.W. The barriers affecting project success. *Proc. 18th Ann. Semin./Symp.* Project Management Institute, Montreal, 1986.

Saint P. Value engineering. *Cost Engr*, 1986, **24**, No. 1, Jan.

Plumb D. Client project execution. *Cost Engr*, 1985, **23**, No. 4, July.

Moore, R.F. *Response to change — the development of non-traditional forms of contracting.* CIOB, 1984.

Morrison M.C. *The management of contracts.* British Institute of Management, London, 1984.

Kharbanda O.P. *et al. Project cost control in action.* Gower, Aldershot, 1983.

O'Riordan T. and Sewell W.R.D. *Project appraisal and policy review.* Wiley, Chichester, 1981.

Marsh P.D.V. *Contracting for engineering and construction projects*, 2nd edn. Gower, Aldershot, 1981.

Project performance reviews

McGettrick S. Improving performance on projects. *MBA Rev. J.*, 1989, **1**, No. 4, December.

Duffy P.J. and Thomas R.D. Project performance auditing. *Project Management J.*, 1989, **7**, No. 2, May.

Pinto J.K. and Stevin D.P. Critical success factors across the project life cycle. *Project Management J.*, 1988, **19**, No. 3, June.

Baker B.M. Lessons learnt from a variety of project failures. *Proc. 9th Wld Congr. Project Management, Glasgow*, 1988.

Ashley D.B. *et al.* Determinants of construction project success. *Project Management J.*, 1987, **18**, June.

Morris P.W.G. and Hough G.H. *Preconditions of success and failure in major projects.* Technical Paper, MPA, 1986.

de Wit A. Measuring project success: an illusion. *Proc. Project Management Inst.*, 1986.

American Society of Civil Engineers. *Management lessons from engineering failures.* K. Gibble (ed.). ASCE, New York, 1986.

Boughey G.E. and Birchell D.W. Auditing of major engineering projects. *Internet Conference, Rotterdam*, 1985.

Ruskin A.M. and Estes W.G. The project management audit: its role and conduct. *Project Management J.*, 1985, June.

General risk management

Cooper D. and Chapman C. *Risk analysis for large projects.* Wiley, Chichester, 1987.

Perry J.G. Risk management — an approach for project managers. *Int. Project Management*, 19864, No. 4, November.

Hayes R.W. *et al. Risk management in engineering construction.* Science and Engineering Research Council (SERC) Project Report, 1987. Distributed by Thomas Telford Ltd, London.

Thomas R.D. Humphreys P.C. and Berkeley D. Project risk action management: techniques and support. Paper presented at

INTERNET International Expert Seminar on The State of the Art in Project Risk Management, Atlanta, GA, October 1989.

Chapman C.B. and Cooper D.F. Risk analysis: testing some prejudices. *European Journal of Operational Research,* **14,** 1983.

Hull J.C. *The evaluation of risk in business investment.* Pergamon, Oxford, 1980.

Risk analysis techniques

Diffenback J. Influence diagrams for complex strategic issues. *Strategic Management Journal,* 1982, **3,** 133–146.

Ashley D.B. and Avots I. Influence diagramming for analysis of project risks. *Int. J. Project Managmenet,* 1984, **15,** No. 1, March, 50–62.

Howard R.A. and Matheson J.E. Influence diagrams. *The principles and applications of decision analysis,* Vol. II (eds Howard and Matheson) Strategic Decisions Group, Merib Park, California, 1984.

Chapman M. Decision analysis. *Civil service college handbook No. 21,* HMSO, London, 1980.

Lifson M.W. and Shaifer E.F. *Decision and risk analysis for construction management.* John Wiley and Sons, New York, 1982.

Albino V. Risk analysis and decision making in engineering processes — a conceptual review of the state of the art. *Proc. 9th INTERNET World Congress on Project Management, Glasgow, 1988.*

Ashley D.B. *et al.* Critical decision making during construction. *Journal Construction Engineering and Management Proc. Am. Soc. Civ. Engrs,* 1983, June.

Jaafari A. Genesis of management confidence techniques. Journal of Management Engineering Proc. Am. Soc. Civ. Engrs, 1987, **3,** No. 1.

Life cycle costing

Flanagan R. and Norman G. *Life cycle for construction.* Royal Institution of Chartered Surveyors, London, 1983.

Stone P.A. *Building design evaluation — costs in use.* Spons, 1967.

Williams G. Costing a packet. *Chartered Quantity Surveyor,* 1987, March.

Ashworth A. Making life cycle costing work. *Chartered Quantity Surveyor,* 1988, April.